THE
ASYMMETRIC
VISION

*Philosophical Intuition and Original Experience
in the Art of Yves Gaucher*

James D. Campbell

Mackenzie Art Gallery

The Asymmetric Vision: Philosophical Intuition and Original Experience in the Art of Yves Gaucher

Mackenzie Art Gallery: Permanent Collection, No. 1

©The contributors and the Norman Mackenzie Art Gallery 1989

Publisher: Norman Mackenzie Art Gallery
          University of Regina
          Regina, Saskatchewan
          Canada, S4S 0A2

Design: Brian Wood Design Studio, Regina

Printing: Houghton Boston, Saskatoon, Saskatchewan, Canada

Photography: All photography is by Pierre Charrier, except plates 8 and 9 by Larry Ostrom, plates 1 and 2 by Don Hall, AV Services, University of Regina, plates 6 and 7 by Al Kilbertus, and the portrait of Yves Gaucher by Richard Max Tremblay.

The monograph has been published by the Norman Mackenzie Art Gallery with support from The Canada Council, Programming Assistance to Public Art Museums and Galleries.

Canadian Cataloguing in Publication Data
Campbell, James D., 1956–
    The asymmetric vision: philosophical intuition and original experience in the art of Yves Gaucher

Bibliography: p. 112
ISBN 0–920922–56–2

    1. Gaucher, Yves, 1934–   . I. Norman Mackenzie Art Gallery.
II. Title.

ND249.G377C34 1989   759.11   C89–090188–0

CONTENTS

Yves Gaucher

Painting is self-discovery. Every good artist paints what he is.
— Jackson Pollock

ILLUSTRATIONS

FOREWORD

The permanent collection is a public art museum's most important resource. A museum's responsibility includes the interpretation of collections for the public as well as collection display, preservation, research, and procurement. Often contemporary concerns in art need fuller explanation to achieve the appreciation they deserve.

With this in mind, the gallery is pleased to launch this publication on eminent Montreal artist Yves Gaucher as the first in a series of short monographs which examine and contextualize single works or groups of work in the collection. The gallery is indeed fortunate to have three of Gaucher's major works in its permanent collection: the intaglio print entitled *En Hommage à Webern #2* of 1963, and the paintings *Signals #2* and *Bruns, Jaune et Rouge* dating from 1966 and 1973 respectively. In his monograph Montreal author James Campbell has located these works within Gaucher's output to date and has clearly enunciated the conceptual and philosophical underpinnings of the artist's abstract style and approach to making art. It has been a pleasure working with Campbell who has also recently written on Canadian contemporary artists Charles Gagnon, Ron Martin, Guido Molinari, and David Rabinowitch; and we would like to acknowledge Philip Monk, Curator of Contemporary Canadian Art, Art Gallery of Ontario, for recommending him to write the text.

This project has been made possible by The Canada Council's Programming Assistance to Public Art Museums and Galleries. We are grateful to James Campbell for his sensitive text and consultations. Finally, we convey our appreciation to the artist Yves Gaucher for his remarkable work.

Andrew Oko
Director

PREFACE AND ACKNOWLEDGEMENTS

It seems entirely appropriate that this series of publications undertaken by the Mackenzie Art Gallery should commence with a monograph on the work of Montreal-based abstract painter Yves Gaucher, long considered one of the foremost artists in this country, whose work continues to go from strength to strength. In this monograph, I try to come to terms with the principal depth-structures of Gaucher's work, reassessing in the process his stellar contribution to contemporary Canadian and international art, and contextualizing and analysing various works at length where they have not received extensive analysis and contextualization in the past.

My mandate and intention here is to briefly survey Gaucher's oeuvre from 1963, discussing in depth those series representative works of which are in the collection of the Gallery, hence focussing on the *Webern* prints, the *Signals/Silences*, and the *Colour Bands*, while discussing other series somewhat less exhaustively, and treating in a certain depth his current work which arguably brings to the highest evolutionary plateau thus far reached those core-themes implicit in the entire body of work.

I begin with a treatment of the role of experience in Gaucher's work. It is my contention that *experience* is lent an awesome primacy in this work which sets it apart from much contemporaneous work. Indeed, it is my belief that experience-as-lived is absolutely crucial to understanding the work in any depth. I go on to discuss notions of intuition, rhythm and asymmetry in the paintings which are grounded in that experience. This is followed by brief treatments of each of the major series Gaucher has executed in the light of these themes. There is a conclusion which stresses the "environmental" nature of this painter's endeavour.

I would like to express my deep gratitude to Andrew Oko, Director of the Mackenzie Art Gallery, for asking me to write this monograph, which inaugurates the series of publications, and to consult on the development of this pilot project. Thus far, it has been a rewarding process. I should point out that while ostensibly serving the purpose of highlighting single works or groups of works in the collection of the Gallery, and thus making that fine collection more widely known, this series serves the wider purpose of affording critics and scholars a forum for in-depth investigations of contemporary work. This is salutary in that the Gallery collection includes many of our leading Canadian artists, from long-established talents like Yves Gaucher to some of our most gifted and acclaimed younger artists like Jeff Wall and Shelagh Alexander.

I would like to thank Mackenzie staff members Bonnie Pedersen

Schaffer, Mary Mahon Jones, Betty Stothers, and others for all their feedback, help and encouragement. I am indebted to the exhaustive and unfailingly lucid scholarship of Dr. Roald Nasgaard, Chief Curator of The Art Gallery of Ontario, Toronto, whose 1978 study entitled *Yves Gaucher: A Fifteen-Year Perspective* still stands as the finest analysis of this artist's work over that period extant. Finally, I would like to thank Yves Gaucher himself, for giving unstintingly of his time in interviews and studio visits throughout the course of my writing this text. He has my lasting gratitude.

James D. Campbell

I.   INTRODUCTION: THE PRIMACY OF EXPERIENCE

A work of art may certainly convey the essence of a multitude of experiences, and sometimes in a remarkably condensed and striking way.

— John Dewey, *Art as Experience*

Yves Gaucher is the consummate example of a contemporary painter who has proposed to set all aesthetic theorizing whatsoever aside in order to pursue, in a pure and unmediated way, his own experience. Rather than pursue the ends of theory, his longstanding methodology has been to imbue his paintings with all the sifted-through "essences" of his own diverse lived-experiences in the world in the act of painting — and few viewers, I think, would begrudge us the judgment here that he has often done so in a remarkably condensed and striking way.

That his paintings are predicated on what has been called the "life-world" and have a direct experiential grounding within it is the necessary premise of the present study. What does "life-world" mean? Simply put: the world of life in which we already live; namely, of human experience as it is concretely lived in the world. And Gaucher's works are not only borne of it but are indissolubly wed to it, find continuing sustenance within it and return us, his observers, to it wholesale in the act of seeing. Thus, Gaucher's philosophy as an abstract painter, as he has himself avowed time and again over the years, is manifestly an *existential* one in which the human agent assumes full responsibility for his own actions and experiences, that is, one in which the observer truly shares in — as opposed to passively surrendering to — the creative act.

Yves Gaucher has always adhered to American philosopher John Dewey's (1859-1952) belief that a work of art's content represents the heightening and intensifying of experiences as lived by the artist. Indeed, Gaucher has studied Dewey's philosophy in depth. Dewey has said: "Instead of fleeing from experience to a metaphysical realm, the material of experiences is so rendered that it becomes the pregnant matter of a new experience."[1] In the context of Gaucher's paintings, that experience is rendered new not only for the artist but for the observer. The essential immanent meanings in his paintings all come from one source: experience. And those meanings become a proverbial wellspring for our own experience. If that seems strange, given the fact that his paintings are resolutely abstract, we can appeal in this regard to his longstanding disdain for theorizing, the fact that he has never had recourse to "fleeing from experience to a metaphysical realm" (being squarely rooted as a painter in his life-world) and the fact that he wants for his own paintings the inborne capacity for inducing those

Plate 1 *Bruns, Jaune et Rouge* 1973

ideas and emotions which are manifestly the fruit of the strongest, if here possibly one of the subtlest, aesthetic experiences. The pre-theoretical intensity of the work is communicated to the observer directly, at a level of generality that allows the widest communion possible; the phenomenal fields of his massive paintings return us to a world of unspoken experience.

In numerous interviews he has granted over the years, Gaucher has always avowed that a given painting is really the sum of his own lived-experiences, whether "listening to an Indian Raga, or jazz, or readings in Eastern and Western philosophies, or playing sports, or even drinking wine or beer . . ."[2] He is not being facetious. He holds that all these things contribute to what a painting is — and not in any mere stylistic sense (for that would be quite impracticable for an artist unwavering in his committment to abstraction). But, more importantly, in the sense of a *state of being*, the sum total of what Yves Gaucher — the artist and the man — was at the time of executing such-or-such a painting. Art, then, *for the artist's sake*, as the poet Charles Baudelaire once articulated it: not for the sake of political messages or aesthetic ploys, or puerile tactics of self-aggrandizement but *art as experience*. While it is probably true that Dewey's objective aesthetic contrasts sharply with the experience of much contemporary abstract art, it is still true that Gaucher was able to derive real inspiration from Dewey's thesis and that experience, at least in his definition, may be said to transcend objective reality altogether.

In these paintings, then, it should be understood from the outset that experience is *the* absolute datum. Not only has it irrevocably shaped the very spirit of what is there on the canvas, within the limits of the unframed picture plane, but the very aspiration to transcend the physicality of the painting is contingent upon it. In other words, whatever emotion a painting like *Bruns, Jaune et Rouge*, of 1973 [pl.1], solicits from us in the act of seeing, it is that induced emotion — whether awe or a pure, unfettered delight — in tandem with the experientially-derived inductive process that went into it, that has any real import or primacy for him as for us, his viewers.

Gaucher wants to render a given painting a world of pure experience and construes, for himself, the surface of a given painting — as well, of course, as its depth-structures — as a dynamic field of experience that is multi-dimensional, open to a plurality of postures and interpretations, and with a plenum of meanings.

It is important to emphasize, I think, that experience as Gaucher understands it for himself as a creative artist is an *ongoing existential process* rather than continuing stasis. Experience is by no means a static process, but a sort of *living dynamism* in which *passage* is the operative word. This is "passage" as Cézanne enigmatically referred to it, having to do with the fidelity of his hand as it followed the most minute shifts in his gaze, imparting to his late oil sketches and watercolors something of the phenomenal ruptures or absences that are created by sundry effects of atmosphere and light. This is passage, too, from one state of mind to another as Gaucher executed and as we regard one of his monumental paintings; that passage from passivity to dynamic response as the painting stakes its claim upon us, as it shapes our experience in the observing and as our imagination become its creative referent.

The brute modes of givenness of paint on canvas — the materiality, the manifest physicality — are always subordinated to or deliberately broken in the attempt to transform *experience* into *painting*, and *painting* into an *experience*, and one accessible to the widest spectrum of possible subjects. A given painting is emphatically more, then, than just the mere sum of its parts. It becomes an entity in its own right, a spiritual entirety, as it were, and one that has been won in and for the *experiencing*. For Gaucher the practising artist, this is finally the only painting methodology that matters, has meaning — or, as he would say, is "worth a damn."

Consequently, we should not be surprised that Gaucher's own formative experiences in painting have less to do with lessons taught by his mentors, the dictates of art theory, the vagaries of style or even the sundry formal demands of asserting a visual language wholly and distinctly his own over the course of more than three decades, than with his own *formative experiences in the life-world*.

It should be noted that Gaucher has travelled extensively. His sorties into China, Mexico and Central America were all crucial life experiences. He studied Islamic architecture in North Africa. Egypt, especially Luxor and Abu Simbel on Lake Nassar, was exceptionally important because it was there that he discovered a concept of monumentality that could inspire genuine awe in the observer; an architecture created by human beings but somehow hard to grasp in human terms. The pyramid of Cheops, the colossi of Ramses the Great at Abu Simbel, the Valley of the Kings, and a host of other Egyptian edifices and locations inspired him. He wanted something of that immeasurable potency for his own paintings. He wanted it as pure and undiluted as possible, without superfluous frills or painterly frolics, and without reducing it to the status of false drama or mere *divertissement*. He wanted it, of course, not as a visual equation in the paintings in any representational sense. Nor as overt content. But in, as he himself avers, "essence".

Gaucher tends to refer to "essences" frequently in conversation and in those few statements he has written over the years. We should not confuse his use of this word with anything like an "absolute idea." That's rubbish. Here is no "mystical vision." If Gaucher's methodology is one of pursuing these essences through what can only be called an intuitive and existential process — as opposed to a wholly analytic or programmatic one beholden to the ends and strictures of theory — this simply means a sort of *methodical clarity in thought* and not by any stretch of the imagination an appropriation from some abstract realm of Platonic forms. Gaucher's "intuition of essences" is an eminently logical process. And, as we shall see presently, it is an eminently empirical one.

Like the trips to Egypt, his sorties into the Mayan cities were nourishing experiences that fructified in essence in his paintings. Whether it be the Monjas Quadrangle at Uxmal or the Red House at Chichén Itzá in the Yucatan, Gaucher has experienced those ancient edifices at first hand, bodily and sensuously, as well as psychologically. "When I was in Tikal, I was experiencing it through the very pores of my body," he has said.[3] He has characterized those sojourns as "rather strong and wondrous existential experiences in which one relates to a whole architecture and seems to radiate more than the sum of what one is."[4] When he returns from one of these trips, he brings back a vast photographic documentation with him, capturing on film the diverse edifices and scenes which he found meaningful and memorable, and which he then selectively filters, reflects upon and collates, effectively "bringing the original past experiences back within my own lived-experience in the present tense."[5] But it should be pointed out that the photographs are not used as reference material for painting, but only as a sort of experiential reservoir that affords Gaucher the opportunity of recalling to memory the specific feelings the sites in question inspired in him. For instance, a photograph taken from the top of the truncated pyramid at Tikal in Gautemala — one of the largest of the Mayan cities, the clouds stretched out at all sides of the pyramid just beneath his eyrie at the pinnacle — registers a standpoint that is still capable of having a continuing impact on him.

If we were to ask ourselves, as observers or, better yet, as *experiencers*, what could possibly relate walking the Jaguar Stairway at Copán or seeing the Acropolis at Piedras Negras for the first time to the experience of observing a painting by Gaucher in any sense more specific than just providing so much experiential fodder for the work, our answer would surely deal with issues of scale and monumentality, and an alternately tangible and elusive spirituality realized in the materials through the staking of a powerfully experiential claim on and through that materiality. The magnetic pull that the Mayan cities exert on all but the most jaded (or jetlagged) individuals has as much to do with their awesome monumentality as with their pervasive aura of mystery. In painting, Gaucher tries to render his materials the meaningful medium for a more transcendent communion with the observer as opposed to creating a mere conduit for conveying a given "message," however glorious or grandiose. Gaucher has a contempt for "easy messages" and has often claimed that, for him, the large scale of his paintings is "as necessary as air" and, in terms particularly of the architecture that has most inspired him, we have no trouble whatsoever understanding why this is so.[6]

As we observe these oversized paintings, we find ourselves poised on the shadow line where the physical structure of a painting and that intangible but somehow coruscating aureole — one may call it the implicit register of the artist's humanity, the peculiar resonances of the painting's "spirituality," or a mastery of chroma, value and hue that is as close to perfect harmony as one can get in the life-world — intersect, cross-fertilize one another, and merge together. Gaucher has staked out for himself this middle ground between an almost ascetic reductivist programme — the reductive process enjoying an absolute primacy from 1963 — in the making of a painting and the primacy of an unalloyed pleasure principle in the assimilating of it. It is a high-wire act and one that requires a consummate sense of balance to bring off. He walks that wire adroitly in his quest for an experiential paradigm: one in paint and on canvas that will be as meaningful for you as it is for me.

This leads us into a discussion of why the phenomenon of "standardization" is wholly anathema to Gaucher, in his painting as in human life. The fact that we are all different, that we emerge from different cultural backgrounds and have divergent ways of thinking about living in our bodies and experiencing our world, is no hindrance to experiencing the paintings, but a very real plus, for Gaucher's project has always been to attempt to articulate the sundry essences and truths of lived-experience in a paradigmmatic way; that is, as I have suggested, in a way that will have a multiplicity of meanings for all possible viewers. Decidedly, then, this is not art wherein "what you see is merely what you see" (and he really discredits that old cliché), not painting in which what is at stake is just the splendid facticity of materials themselves or so many splendorous messages. But the lived-register of a real and vital urge towards transcendence. And painting, for him, its one inviolable vehicle.

So, while resolutely empirical in one limited sense, the work nonetheless provides a real incentive to contemplation. I mean contemplation in the experiential sense in which John Dewey meant it, as "designating that aspect of perception in which elements of seeking and of thinking are subordinated (although not absent) to the perfecting of the process of perception itself."[7] Contemplation in this sense does not imply a static process or some monkish state of withdrawal from a painting in order to know it, but the active presence of desire and thought in the perceiving of it, while recognizing it as a continuing stimulus — and in perfecting that process of perception to the greatest possible extent.

As we stand before *Signals #2* of 1966 (pl. 2) and let it work its magic upon us, as we allow it to speak in its own voice, so low and meditative at one moment, so rhythmic and hypnotic the next, as we let it articulate itself in its own space, in its own time, we experience something quite ineffable, rife with unearthly inflections of hue and subtle tonal nuances, that is an experience in its own right, and one at once quite similar to and distinct from those experiences we ordinarily live.

In my title to this monograph, I refer to the "original" experience implicit in his paintings. It is "original" not only because it takes a cue from the original rhythms of nature but, more importantly perhaps, because it is not *dehumanized*. Its origins reside in experience. It has been purified in the aesthetic realm yet it has successfully broken the hold of the *a priori* in its fidelity to lived-experience and existential presence. In this sense it is no different, then, in itself, from our own privileged experiences in the life-world. But it is also *original* in the sense of bearing the imprimatur of the unique character of the artist's own lived-through world experience.

Take again, in this context, *Signals #2*, in which the perceived emanation of a preternatural deep quiet, the pulse that begins, as if in the veins of one's own body, that ebbs and flows in the mind, and in time, seems to build up a slow, magisterial rhythm akin to the sinuous movements of an Indian raga or the more tensile passages of a Sonny Rollins saxophone solo. It may not be considered appropriate to some to liken the experience of looking at a painting by Yves Gaucher to the experience of listening to the work of a musician who was likened more than once to a Picasso of the saxophone (interestingly, Rollins started out as a painter), but it seems to this writer, intuitively, very telling and very apt.

And, while albeit perhaps stretching my analogy to the breaking-point, it must be said that it does seem that Rollins the saxophonist enjoys somewhat the same freedom — and achieves the same level of excellence — by playing without a harmonic base as Gaucher does when he is painting in "deep asymmetry." Real harmonic and rhythmic freedom is a rare thing, indeed, and is to be savored particularly when themes are broken down and manipulated with such dexterity and fluid formal integrity that they literally take your breath away.

In the case of Gaucher's painting, whether it be a feeling of outright awe, the inception of a sort of inward silence, or the harbinger of some hallucinatory clarity, it stakes a powerful experiential claim upon us, both psychic and somatic, that is hard to gainsay or dismiss. When British curator and critic Bryan Roberston said that Gaucher: "is making what are possibly the most beautiful and original — and awe-inspiring — paintings I've seen anywhere since the advent of Pollock and Rothko" he was voicing just how moved he was by the experiential integrity and aesthetic achievement of Gaucher's work, and attesting, above all, to the strength of the claim we have discussed.[8]

At their best, Gaucher's paintings ensure that we have the experience and *not* miss the meaning, that sudden illumination that limns the threshold of our awareness, instilling a sort of awe, and which then in turn transforms that experience (which began, of course, as a purely aesthetic experience) beyond any meaning we can assign to such experience. It is deepened and directed to the pre-objective from one tense to the next and back again. As we shall see, it is precisely through his continuing search for living rhythms communicable through the paired syntaxes of symmetry and asymmetry that the real meaning of his work emerges and any meaningful experience of it is made possible.

Plate 2   *Signals #2*   1966

II.   INTUITION, RHYTHM, ASYMMETRY

Gaucher has often been called an "intuitive" painter. The label is appropriate but I would like to define it here with rather more specificity that
has ordinarily been the case. It seems plain to the understanding that
Gaucher's intuitions are the intuitions of a very gifted painter but that,
far more than this, they are "philosophical" in nature. What could that
mean? If the patient reader will bear with me for a moment, I would
like to clarify this further.

The thinker Emmanuel Levinas once claimed:

> Philosophical intuition is not, as in Bergson's philosophy or in
> the 'philosophies of life', an act in which all the vital forces are
> engaged, an act which plays an important role in the destiny
> of life. Philosophical intuition is a reflection on life considered
> in all its concrete fullness and wealth, a life which is considered
> but no longer lived.[9]

This definition is an exact one for Gaucher's own working methodology. His process of reflecting in his paintings is directed towards the
plenitude and distilled richness of his own experience first, and he
strives to imbue the paintings with that richness mediated by the purity
and the open parameters of his chosen formal syntax, and his reduced
means, and while it can "no longer be lived" by him in a literal sense,
having taken its cue from experience already lived, it can, however, be
lived very satisfactorily by the observer again and again in front of any
one of his majestic paintings.

This ties in with his intuitions being directed towards things "in their
essences" in the process of painting and which I referred to earlier. The
whole business of intuiting "essences" has a long philosophical history.
But when I call his intuitions "philosophical" and note his preoccupation with "essences" here I do not wish to invoke that history in its
specificity, which some would call archaic or unfounded in the present
context. I am merely reminding the reader that Gaucher's signature
"intuitive process" has as many *logical* underpinnings as it does *poetic*
overtones and adamantly partakes more of the *empirical* than it does
of the *metaphysical*. The "essences" in question always derive from experience. The "isness" or beingness of a given painting derives from
those essences. Gaucher's methodology may be intuitive, but as a working manifestation of progressive clarification and thought it is also
highly empirical, and continually returns to its previous stages and
formal problems in order to achieve the clarification of foundations
and concepts and the more thorough investigation of problems that
works in earlier series may have necessarily left unclarified or unresolved

at that point. Even if something has been confronted directly but its ramifications have lain fallow for say, five, ten, twenty years, Gaucher will inevitably return to it and explore those ramifications methodically.

It is necessary to emphasize this because so many people still mistakenly believe that "intuition," when referred to in aesthetic discourse, necessarily rules out the workings of rigorous logic or the systematic elucidation of a given problem. In the sense used here, intuition does not necessarily exclude the intellect or logic — or the "theory" in the sense in which Gaucher's formal syntax has laid down distinct attributes and parameters over the course of some thirty years — but achieves an altogether harmonic balance with them in the ongoing process of making paintings.

This ties in with Gaucher's longstanding avowal that intuition, for him, alternately fuels and feeds on one's acquired store of knowledge. The more knowledge one has, the more intuitive one can be. The findings afforded by intuition cycle through the whole process because intuition is transformed into knowledge and vice-versa. Intuition, then, is not an end in itself, but a dynamic ethic that affords the artist a fruitful ground for his working methodology and a vital source for replenishing his formal language and its experiential and epistemological roots.

One might suggest — and I do so here with all due caution for it may seem a truism or even too intrepid to some but must, in any case, be stated boldly — that the principal philosophical intuition that Gaucher the abstract painter has is one, and perhaps strangely (given his chosen idiom), of the *life of others*. For, while his syntax is wholly abstract, the empathic force of his painting is inordinately strong, and grounded in this life-world we all share. While this could once be said apropos so much contemporary work, I would contend that it takes on a wholly new and contemporaneous meaning in this oeuvre, wherein *sharing* is an active state. Empathy, after all, and contrary to a supposition common among some commentators, is not predicated on or limited purely to figurative art alone. Gaucher's work has what can be only called an "organic resonance" that enhances its accessibility even if it is one that, starting with the *Webern* prints, is posited by an implicit *phenomenology of perception* rather than, as was the case with the relief prints executed before 1963, an *explicit language of organic form*.

This ties in with Gaucher's belief, oft-expressed, that a totalizing objectivity, aesthetically-speaking, is simply not possible because that would involve a standardizing of everybody's experience. He holds that we live in a subjective world first, before living in that "objective" and supposedly true world that is based on and is being continuously buttressed by the objectivating norms of modern science. But the former, the subjective world, is the only one capable of being truly experienced. Hence, we may say with some justification that it is the only true world.[10] This deeply- and even fiercely-held belief is reflected in all Gaucher's work, whether it be painting, drawing or printmaking.

In contemporaniety, this is far more controversial than it may at first seem. For we are living in a time when the discourse of the "subject" is commonly held to be archaic; a discourse, in effect, to be disavowed altogether in favor of some more fashionable alternative. This is especially true with respect to painting and the critical apparatus that besieges it on all sides. For Gaucher, the notion of or the necessity for an absent or "decentered" subject is absolutely meaningless; or, perhaps, absolutely meaningful. Why? If we have recently seen in art and attendant criticism a radical displacement of the subject, then Gaucher, particularly in his current paintings, demonstrates that such a displacement really opens up a space in which the subject can be radically restored, and effectively transvalued. For the whole focus of his work has been on shifting the onus from the context of what could have been an otherwise empty formalism onto layers and layers of lived-experience, and *sans* the claims of the ego (the emphasis on the experiential always eclipsing the egocentric expression, thus instituting a sort of humanism), and then on peeling those layers away like the multiple skins of an onion, to reach cardinal essences which are first constituted in paint and on canvas, for the sole purpose of their being reconstituted by any number of different observers, an open set of other restored subjectivities.

In some revealing remarks dating as early as 1965, Gaucher stressed the importance of a "visual rhythm" in his work. He has said:

> I don't think rhythm is a musical term. I think it is a term of life. That's an entirely different ball game. Rhythm is basically a recurrence of elements in time — as loosely as that. Then it envelops a whole cyclic thought — night and day, night and day, and night and day. The four seasons coming back is rhythm. The heart beat is rhythm. The cycle of the moon is a rhythmic cycle. The cycle of life and death is a rhythmic cycle.[11]

We can see from these remarks that Gaucher conceives of rhythm as having far more universality than just its privileged status in music; he believes it is a "term of life." More importantly, perhaps, it is a *lebensformen*, that is, a *form of life*. Indeed, in this larger sense his concern with rhythm dovetails neatly with John Dewey's stress on the importance of rhythm in art — and takes a certain inspiration from this philosopher's arguments. Dewey has argued:

> Interaction of environment with organism is the source, direct or indirect, of all experience and from the environment come those checks, resistances, furtherances, equilibria which, when they meet with the energies of the organism in appropriate ways, constitute form. The first characteristic of the environing world that makes possible the existence of artistic form is rhythm. There is rhythm in nature before poetry, painting, architecture and music exist. Were it not so, rhythm as an essential property of form would be merely superimposed upon material, not an operation through which material effects its own culmination in experience.[12]

This is a truth that Gaucher the practising artist understands very well. Rhythm is the phenomenon through which this artist's material — paint applied in a seemingly impersonal manner to lengths of cotton duck canvas — effects its own culmination in the experience of the observer. This artist's specific genius has been to seek after the rhythm in modes of thematic asymmetry, harmonic decomposition and structural contrariety rather than solely in and through the syntax of dynamic symmetry. His work seems to oscillate between symmetry and asymmetry with an unusual and telling periodicity — "telling" because the truth is that Gaucher always returns to symmetry when he wants to define the parameters of a problem he needs to solve. Symmetry is used methodologically as a way to learn the rules and principles involved before being able to break them and lend them new, hitherto unseen significance through recourse to asymmetry. Asymmetry is thus a way "to open up the enquiry rather than continuing to deal with problems you know."[13] Once having defined the parameters of the problem, it is never long before he plunges once again into the realm of complexity or "chaotic dynamics," as he himself calls that topography of partial or total asymmetry.[14] It is also interesting to note that asymmetry always has its departure in a particular use of symmetry; that asymmetry always commences, for Gaucher, in symmetric structures, before expressing itself in structures that are wholly asymmetric.

This explains, in effect, largely why his work is so unconventional — and perhaps helps us understand why it can be so moving. He is able to attain virtually "perfect pitch" in the syntax of dynamic asymmetry. This is something which invariably captivates the attention of his observers in a phenomenal way, because it departs so far from the

strictures of a more conventional visual language, but never stops short
of promising the spectator a kind of rapture.

Shortly after Gaucher executed his *En Hommage à Webern* prints in
1963, he executed an unpublished print (fig. 1) which explicitly posits
the problem of asymmetry that became increasingly important from
one *Webern* print to the next. The diagonal is comprised of a number
of right angles, that are sequentially inverted as they rhythmically
progress in a line of dynamic tension from bottom left to top right. This
important print, never before reproduced in any text on Gaucher's
oeuvre, clearly establishes an early and vital manifestation of this artist's
"asymmetric vision" and a first, strong statement of the diagonal.

Fig. 1   *Untitled*   1963

Gaucher articulated his quest for visual rhythm more extensively in
a little-known but important statement published to accompany an
exhibition of paintings at Gallery Moos in Toronto in 1966 (and, it should
be noted, Gaucher has written very few statements over the years, prefer-
ring the work to speak for itself), in which he explicitly mentions the
importance of a "visual rythmics." It is worth quoting in its entirety here:

> Each language in art speaks an idiom that conveys what cannot
> be said in any other without loss of meaning. This principle has

finally become factual in painting; therefore, a probing knowledge of visual and plastic realities and its application to a significantly structured and precise idiom is imperative: a profound transformation of our attitudes to the substance and logic of perceptual mechanisms is also required.[15]

In this early statement, Gaucher indicates the necessity for a precise "idiom" that would be wholly and distinctly his own. He continues, outlining his programme as follows:

(1) the development of chromatic antagonisms in colour-perception, (2) the dynamic logic of the contradictory in structural relationships, and (3) the empirical development of "visual rhythmics" through the usage of principles of 'relations of indetermination' have become my motive.[16]

Certainly, Gaucher has explored at some length the possibility of chromatic antagonisms in colour-perception but never, it should be stressed, as an alienating device (as was arguably the case with Op Art). Indeed, it is often by developing chromatic antagonisms in the subtlest possible fashion that Gaucher is able to achieve an unearthly chromatic and harmonic composition and decomposition. One might cite, in this regard, his current paintings which proffer colours we have never seen before in our life-world (a bold claim, perhaps, but the reader is challenged to observe his current series of *Pale Paintings*, and decide the matter for himself/herself) and in colour and spatial relationships which should not work but nevertheless do work. As for the *dynamic logic of the contradictory* in structural relationships, Gaucher is referring here to his thematic, if simply unthematized, use of structural contrariety, *asymmetry*, "relations of indetermination" and "chaotic dynamics." Finally, concerning the need for the "empirical development of a 'visual rythmics'" this is something that has marked his work from 1963 to the present. Gaucher's statement concludes:

Involvement in these attitudes requires a modification of the notion of natural elements into 'energetic events' — the complex factors of visual experience. This modification is essential for the continued germination of my art; it tends to define the visual language in its purest sense, thus giving it greater scope and clarity. We are living an intense period of research and discovery: if my art is to be the manifestation of such a time, then it is imperative that the language used be parallel to the statement intended.[17]

Gaucher's concern that "the language used be parallel to the statement intended" is one that animates the whole oeuvre. He has never forsaken it in favor of a less demanding methodology. Indeed, the visual language he has chosen to use is so phenomenally meshed and in continuing synchronicity with his own intentionality — the claims, that is, of his own experience — that any attempt to separate them off would be pure folly.

The philosopher Mikel Dufrenne has written on the role of rhythm in painting in a way that seems strikingly apt for Gaucher's work:

> . . . movement [in painting] is ordered by rhythm and thus manifests a duration which is born of the animation of space. It is true that rhythm can animate only space. It cannot inscribe a real becoming in objective time. Rhythm does not preside over a temporal progression but over the unification of a spatial manifold. Yet space in this case is no longer the inert space of geometry. It has become a field of action where something happens, contrasts are resolved, and conflicts arise and pass away. As a result, rhythm is here inseparable from harmony, whereas in music the two can be kept separate if necessary.[18]

In one sense, this is precise for the spatiality of Gaucher's painting. It is never the space of an empty geometry but a space in which something transpires, is experientially-derived (despite the fact that it is wholly non-mimetic) and, thus, a space in which *felt transcendence* is possible. Where he departs from Dufrenne's statement, however, pertains to the issues of rhythm not being able to "inscribe a real becoming in objective time" and with respect to rhythm being inseparable from harmony. First of all, Gaucher has always been preoccupied with the durational temporality of his work. He wanted to create paintings that would, in effect, reorganize themselves in front of the observer throughout the duration of one's experience. Gaucher has likened the effect to that of music but notes that music is predetermined, whereas his own paintings celebrate openness, freedom from the tyranny of predetermined schemas, and a sheer plenum of meanings. This "duration" is a block of time in which the observer becomes a creative participant in the work; that is, wherein the onus for constituting the work shifts over to the observer who takes on the status of a "creator" who must complete the work within his/her own sensibility and body-schema. As to the latter issue, it is here that the artist's vital kinship with music can be seen only too well, for rather frequently throughout the work we will be investigating here, Gaucher preserves a rhythmic schema in a given painting even when inordinately complex and seem-ingly incompatible colour-schemas seem to deny all possibility of a harmonic base.

This is because the rhythmic schemata of Gaucher's paintings are not invested in just the vagaries of spatial organization or even in the har-monic schemas of colour but in a *space of action*. Obviously, rhythms can be found in his paintings which are purely symmetric; but one might with some justification suggest the most vital and moving rhythms are in those works which can be classified as being purely asymmetric.

What Eugène Delacroix suggestively called "the music of the picture" is always waiting to be discovered in a painting by Gaucher, whether it be one of the prints circa 1963 or one of the current paintings of 1989. And it is a music that woos us just as relentlessly as it awakens us to a realm of experience quite unqualified, unwritten in the annals of more conventional aesthetic experience and "subsequent attrition."

Gaucher's "asymmetric vision" is grounded in Delacroix's "music" as much as it is grounded in ordinary experience. The music in question is, in any case, the very music of our experience. And we should remem-ber that, in the life-world, the pull of gravity itself renders the space we inhabit wholly asymmetrical. Rudolf Arnheim has discussed this at length, and the way in which he discusses it has real implications for the perception of Gaucher's paintings, particularly the *Colour Bands*:

> Human beings experience the dynamic asymmetry or aniso-tropy of space by means of two senses, kinesthesis and vision. Kinethesis, the sense that reports on the physical tensions active in the body, inteprets gravitational pull as weight. Physically, gravitational pull and weight are the same thing; perceptually, they are different. Perceptually, weight is normally not attri-buted to the attractive power of a distant center but experienced as a property of the object itself. The object is perceived kinesthetically as an independent center to which we attribute heaviness. It is experienced not as being pulled, but as press-ing downward.[19]

The monumental scale of Gaucher's paintings is necessary for the apprehension and abiding articulation of the dynamic asymmetry of "gravitational space." As we stand in front of one of his monumental paintings, we experience in our bodies and through the mechanisms of our optic a genuine surrogate for the anisotropy of space.

This is precisely what Gaucher strives after. For him, the only reality is experience. This is perhaps the *sine qua non* of what I have chosen to call his "asymmetric vision." Indeed, we could take all this one quantum stage further and point out that the relation between reality and experience is itself basically asymmetrical. And this relation, as Erazim Kohak has pointed out:

> ... is not a matter of philosophical speculation but of *ordinary experience*. Reality must be experienceable, but experience does not similarly require a factual component. Even without it, it still retains all its basic structures. Fear, joy, guilt, lived through in a dream or vicariously in fiction, experienced in memory or in anticipation, are recognizably the same experience as when they are lived by the waking cogito. [My italics][20]

This is exactly Gaucher's own best sentiment; one that effectively closes the gap as much on our side as on his side — for we are all *experiencers* — between *experiencing* and *painting*. Kohak points out that much of the appeal of literature rests in its capacity to make us live through "a range of human experiences which have no factual counterparts in our lives."[21] This is exactly what Gaucher wants for his painting: to make it an engine for running experiences which may have no factual counterparts in our lives but which are nonetheless very real — and very moving. That he accomplishes this more often than not (and uncompromisingly so) attests to the experiential integrity of the work and the strength of those philosophical intuitions that are its true underpinnings. Because, while Kohak is correct in judging that the relation between reality and experience is not an issue of "philosophical speculation" it still requires philosophical intuitions to sort it all out, whether in writing or on canvas. We should remember that Gaucher has often referred to himself as a "philosopher." He has said it in a half-joking, half-serious way. But he is, indeed (if qualifiedly) a philosopher; that is, one with a paintbrush.

III.   THE WEBERN PRINTS

The year 1963 marks an early watershed in the evolution of Gaucher's work. It was during this year that he executed a suite of three remarkable intaglio prints entitled *En Hommage à Webern*. [pls. 3,4,5] The importance of these works was recognized from the outset. They were first exhibited at the Martha Jackson Gallery in New York, in November, 1963.

When Gaucher left Montréal's Ecole des Beaux Arts in 1960, he purchased his own intaglio press, and began a long period of print experimentation, particularly with embossing. While he had studied printmaking at school, most notably under the tutelage of Albert Dumouchel (1916-1971), it was the period of being on his own, maturing as an artist unselfconsciously and experimenting freely without the constraint of academic rules and entrenched ways of doing things, that resulted in the *Webern* prints. Gaucher devoted himself exclusively to printmaking in the period between 1961 and 1964.

He made a series of real breakthroughs in his printmaking during those years that represented far more than just tacit familiarity with the medium and processes involved. His sundry technical innovations — such as his particular use of indented and raised relief — were acclaimed as remarkable for that time (indeed, they won him prestigious national and international awards); but, by no means unprecedented in the history of his own work, although they do embody a concrete and remarkable synthesis of his concerns, innovations and techniques in printmaking up to that date.

Gaucher travelled to Paris in 1962 and attended a concert that spotlighted compositions by Anton Webern, the early twentieth-century Viennese composer who pioneered, along with Arnold Schoenberg, serial music. Specifically, Webern's "Opus # 5 for Small Orchestra" and "The Six Bagatelles for String Quartet" moved him. Indeed, it would be an understatement to suggest that these compositions made a considerable impact upon Gaucher, so indelibly did those sounds impress themselves on his aural memory, becoming somehow visual or, better, suggesting the possibility of a visual experience as radical in its own way as his experience of the sounds was.

Gaucher was not "naïf" as far as music was concerned at this stage in his life. He knew jazz, Indian and classical music quite well, and had even played some instruments (although he was prepared to admit to me recently he recognized early that he was a "bad musician").[22] But the Webern concert was galvanizing because, as he says, it "challenged every single idea I had about sound, about art, about expression, about the dimensions all these things could have. And I was extremely disturbed."[23] Concerning the composition itself, Gaucher described how

Plate 3   *En Hommage à Webern, 1*   1963

"the music seemed to send little cells of sound into space, where they expanded and took on a whole new quality and dimension of their own."[24]

Gaucher, trying to describe to me the experience once again after having given so many accounts over the years, said that it was like "sound cells being lobbed into empty space and exploding like firecrackers . . .The experience was profoundly moving."[25] This is so reminiscent of his prior remarks that we can see that, even after so many years, the experience has not appreciably dimmed for him in remembered intensity. Gaucher once commented apropos these prints: "They have contained a lot more than I could tackle [at once], a lot of ingredients that would become mine over a period of time."[26]

However, as several commentators have pointed out, these prints were not Gaucher's first real accomplishment, although they are certainly the most accomplished work to that date and qualify as a real watershed. Gaucher had already had a one-man show at the Galerie L'Echange in Montreal in 1957. His work had already been included in a number of prestigious international exhibitions. He had received important awards for his prints and his work was already represented in several significant public and private collections.

Experience invariably leads to introspection, then to analytic and synthetic activity, and this to significant *innovation*, in Gaucher's working methodology. Experience is *always* the catalyst. While this may be a truism of much artwork, it is still particularly true of Gaucher's work in general, and of the *Weberns* particularly.

In the six months between hearing the Webern concert and executing the prints, Gaucher executed hundreds of tiny drawings in which the signature motifs — the squares and short linear elements — of the *Weberns* first emerge amongst a litany of residual organic forms with which the pre-Webern prints are rife. At this point, Gaucher was in the studio twelve hours each and every day. In hindsight, he remembers that it was an incredibly intense period of work and, in fact, one of the most intense working periods of his adult life. The small drawings and contemporaneous prints reflect that intensity. They constitute a sort of graphic, progressively geometrically-oriented shorthand in which small rectilinear blocks begin to appear coupled with linear elements, right angles and so forth in a larval iconography as cryptic and condensed as it is kinetically-charged. These drawings are clearly indicative of Gaucher's attempt to provoke a language shorn of any nuance of figuration, and one as pared down as possible, decidedly minimal without being at all "minimalist." (Indeed, Gaucher's disdain for minimalism,

Op Art, and art-movements of every stripe is rather vociferous and widely-known.)

In this sense, the evolution of drawings and prints over this period also bears telling witness to the reductive character of this artist's whole process, with its emphasis on progressively stripping away everything he feels is superfluous to the formal integrity of his work's core-features. Finally, in the *Weberns,* he is left with a bare handful of highly reduced elements capable of acting in alternately symphonic and atonal concert on the white surface of the paper, seemingly freely dispersed but in fact positioned according to a grid format, albeit a barely perceptible one.

Roald Nasgaard has argued, with some justification, that:

> The prints thus consitute a variety of geometric abstraction, but it is important to notice that the individual compositional elements function less as integral shapes than they do as graphic stimuli guiding eye movements. We might call them visual cues, or "signals," though only in 1966 would Gaucher adopt the latter term.[27]

These impressions in relief on laminated paper are sparsely populated with either tiny uncoloured or heavily inked coloured squares, lines and right angles in positive or negative relief. One recalls the later compositions of Piet Mondrian and it is as though the coloured squares in a painting like *Broadway Boogie-Woogie* are dynamically transposed and pushed one step further, sinking perceptibly into or achieving perceptible frontality within the backdrop space. Each square seems, then, perfectly poised within that space, whether floating upon its surface or somehow instantiated within it.

The first print (pl. 3) is comprised of large, implied yet incomplete planar shapes in which the lines, once suggested, are reiterated across the overall plane, just as the elements in Anton Webern's compositions are reiterated in accelerating harmonic contrast. In other words, while the overall placement seems to be random, in fact it is not at all random. There is no colour save black and grey in this print.

The second print (pl. 4) is increasingly asymmetric. The asymmetry can be perceived in the contrast between its energized left side and somewhat empty right side. Gaucher has said, in this respect, that the second print is arguably the most important of the three for what he calls the "suppleness through the diagonals."[28] Gaucher introduces negative relief. There is also a latent triangular format. The triangles are the very basis for the diagonals.

Plate 4   *En Hommage à Webern, 2*   1963

There is a distinct development in the three prints which is more intuitive than programmatic, a tendency towards progressive asymmetry. Structurally speaking, *Webern #2* started in a similar way to *Webern # 1* with the placing of lines that were supposed to be extensions of their forerunners but actually were not. When I suggest that there is nothing programmatic or preordained — and this is something quite different from suggesting that overall composition is not random — about these works, it is entirely in keeping with Gaucher's approach, which is precisely to establish a theory and then push beyond it, deconstruct it as one faces the end results of one's own assumptions in the process. For Gaucher theorizing is synonymous with taxonomy, which he would find a real hindrance in the evolutive process of his works. Here, *excessive definition* means *limitation,* and that destroys the ongoing process. This self-questioning has always been a hallmark of his practice.

In the third print (pl. 5), the asymmetric thrust across the whole plane is carried out through an implied diagonal which runs from the upper left to the lower right. Triangles appear again in the sense of discrete squares which are readable, configurationally-speaking, as a triangular motif. In this print, relations of indetermination powerfully emerge.

Within the strongly implied but still hypothetical grid structure of all three prints, the visual cells seem kinetically attracted and repelled — like the positive and negative fields generated by a magnet in relation to which iron filings attract or repulse each other, so that the space between them is charged with an invisible energy — keeping the line of dynamic tension through the print taut, giving an impression of absolute and exquisite rightness of placement, and subtending lateral tensions to all peripheries of the sheet.

As Nasgaard has pointed out, the purpose of the embossing is to frustrate any facile illusionistic reading of the space of the paper.[29] But it is also an attempt to free the observer from the limitations of being bound to the picture plane in the process of seeing, to push out into a real space so that the observer must contend with the relief motifs on another level. As we shall see, this is the same effect he has sought throughout his career, and which he has once again achieved in the dematerializing spatiality of his current *Pale Paintings*.

These prints should really be understood as snares for the enquiring eye; as magnets or traps for perception, forcing our eyes to rove across the surface restlessly from one configuration to the next, seeking out some final *gestalt* that will order the whole composition and lend it final, cohesive meaning. But they never resolve into an easily-won stasis. Instead, they resolutely defeat all implications of closure.

Here we barely glimpse the underlying grid pattern, the implied completion of angles in some final symmetrical placement, only to have our desire frustrated at the last instant and our optic pitched back once again into the fray, which has suddenly become wholly asymmetric and resists any easy classification.

It was by shifting the focus wholesale onto the experience of the observer that Gaucher was to prefigure in this work his career-long preoccupation with the status — the role and the perceptual *experience* — of the observer. Even at this early stage in his career, he demonstrated how he could transcend the physical givenness of the print, its materiality, in placing the emphasis on the *meaning* of lived-experience for the observer. Gaucher's shifting of this constitutive onus from his own experience to the experiential processing of the print itself on the part of the spectator — that is, from the aesthetic object itself onto the perceptual processes that will receive and codify it — in the *Weberns* would become by no means unprecedented in the wider context of post-1960s production, but is certainly remarkable at this time, and remarkable on several other counts as well, mainly having to do with the kinetic byproducts of a visualizing structure of asymmetry. As we have seen, that visualizing structure of asymmetry is meaningfully imbued in much of his work.

I think Nasgaard was right in adjudging most commentators as being somehow at fault in seeking so assiduously for formal influences in modern music to explain the radicality of these *Webern* prints and their thematic set of concerns.[30] While it is true that music has always been of great importance to Gaucher, it has never appreciably impacted on his *style* as a visual artist but has at best suggested analogous ways of thinking in visual terms, intentionally and methodologically-speaking, that represented something as radical and majestic for him as the aural experience.

On the the other hand, I think it should be stressed that when a commentator has recourse to a musical metaphor in writing on Gaucher — and the reader will have occasion to witness the having of such recourse many times in this text — I think it is perfectly appropriate. Why? Because the contemplative nature of Gaucher's enterprise sounds certain grace notes so epiphanous, subtle, and hauntingly elusive that perhaps only music provides writers with a valid parallel for or worthy equivalent of that experience.

Doris Shadbolt, to cite just one instance, compares the *Weberns* to twelve tone music: "a kind of composing in which the initial set of notes, once chosen and ordered, becomes a 'toy' which the composer can send

Plate 5 *En Hommage à Webern, 3* 1963

into space, allow to expand and 'play.' Webern's mathematically precise, highly intellectual and ordered world was sympathetic to Gaucher in general, and in particular the idea of performing, of having a set or structure of relationship from which to expand, struck home. From this time on his work, which was already distinctly thematic in nature, each cluster sharing a common pictorial and technical idea, was to become more consciously and rigorously serial in nature."[31] Yet, Gaucher maintains today that he used musical references in his titles "only so that people could better understand the work in the absence of any storyboard." And that while he wanted a visual structure that could be as pure in its own way as the music of Webern, Varese or Boulez, "the problem is that people took things far too literally! It is emphatically not a visual music. It does, however, have rhythm. But rhythm is not just a musical term."[32] As we have seen earlier, it is, in effect, a "form of life."

The *Weberns* were followed by a several other important laminated prints, including *Fugue Jaune* (1963), *Pli Selon Pli* (1964), *Espace Activé* (1964) and *Point Counterpoint* (1965). The latter is notable in directly fore-telling the field-structure of the *Signals/Silences* paintings of 1966.

The *Weberns* are significant as much for what they visualize as for what they portend, for all the important subsequent themes of his oeuvre are there at the outset: the pursuit of rhythms, the concern for dura-tion, the methodological significance of the reductive process, the movement from symmetry to asymmetry, and the primary roles of expe-rience and philosophical intuition.

IV.   DANSES CARRÉES [SQUARE DANCES]

In 1964, Gaucher returned to painting after a lengthy hiatus in which he had focussed exclusively on his printmaking and, at first glance, his painting seems to represent a real departure from the themes he had been pursuing in the prints. But appearances can be misleading, at least in this case, and Gaucher was really exploring those same themes with sustained rigor but from a different perspective and with a different purpose in the paintings. The print entitled *Espace Activé*, with its extensive use of colour and complex structuration, directly foretells the concerns that Gaucher would address in these paintings. At this point in time, Gaucher was driven to create a colour-field for intervention, rather than the white field of the prints, and has said that this print specifically impelled him back to paint.

The *Danses Carrées* were executed in a square format (turned 45 degrees) like Mondrian's co-called "lozenges." The title means literally "square dances" and seems highly appropriate, given the relentless and kinetic energy of these works. They emphasize total symmetry. In this series, thematic motifs include linear elements of approximately the same length and small diamonds set against coloured backdrops in relation to which their own colours have been modified accordingly to produce certain optical effects, such as after-image. But never spasmodic after-image, and not necessarily yielding extreme optic fatigue or the distantiating effects of extreme "dazzle."

Yet, in this respect, the *Danses Carrées* remind us, by virtue of their strongly implied, structurally kinetic rhythmic movements, of the so-called "rotating trapezoidal window" in studies of perceptual learning in which a given subject viewed a rotating trapezoid enclosing white-mullioned plane surfaces with painted shadows so as to represent a three-dimensional window. Those studies found that there were striking phenomena apropos subjects' perceptions related to shape assumptions, and perceived movement.[33] The ambiguous cues of motion parallax are perfectly analogous for what the viewer experiences in observing the field structures of a given *Danse Carrée* painting by Gaucher, for example *Danse Carrée* of 1965 (pl. 6).

I do not want to render that experience scientific, however, which would only make it untrue for the work in question. The "lozenge" carries what can only be characterized as an "erotic" surcharge, which is part and parcel of its kinesics, and which portends a tonic exhilaration of the senses for the observer. This effect is remarkable in that Gaucher, as he always has, applied his paint to the canvas with rigorous pictorial economy and a standard roller in order to prevent the sensibility or gestural presence of the hand from interfering with the

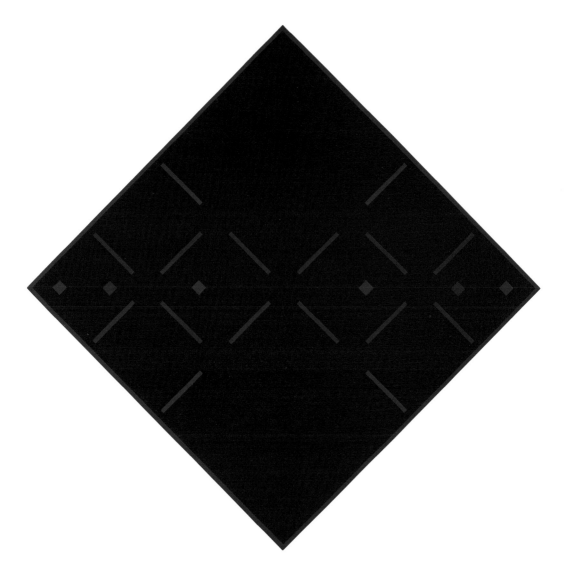

Plate 6   *Danse Carrée*   1965

perceptual purity of the colour-field itself and thus effectively fore-stalled the intervention of the authority of a purely autobiographical consciousness. Yet we do respond to the work with the full complicity of the body: through its kinesthesis, its libidinal strivings, its body-image and its incarnation or concrete placement in a world.

Gaucher has referred to this series as being a purely transitional one *en route*, as it were, towards something else, i.e., as a way of finding himself in paint and colour. But it is nonetheless an important chapter in the history of his work. It demonstrates his concern with the experience of the observer. It is worth noting that the transitional aspect of this work has less to do with the issue of manifest content than with its apparently absolute symmetry *vis à vis* the preceding prints wherein the emphasis was clearly on a movement towards increasing asymmetry.

Commentator Gerald Needham has eloquently summarized the relation of these works to the relief prints that directly preceded them:

> After the relief prints, the appearance of the big diamond-shaped paintings of 1965 must have been startling. Yet the latter are in some ways only a staightforward reversal of the elements of the prints. In the prints the shape of the work and the colour are unimportant, the composition is asymmetrical, and while the size is small the movement extends well beyond the picture edges. It is the opposite in the large symmetrical *Danses Carrées:* the diamond shape of the canvas is unforgettable and colour is crucial, while the energy is mainly contained within the canvas (whirling square dancers always threaten to fly off into space but are held in their patterns).[34]

It should be noted, however, that there is finally nothing whatsoever of Op Art about these marvellously kinetic paintings, which manage to subvert their own symmetry through the relentless dynamism and circularity of their rhythms, which can be likened to a serpent chasing its tail around the central axis, and, as a matter of fact, giving rise to some of the same symbolic associations. The afterimages induced by an intense experience of colour and form in a state of perennial decomposition do not confuse, dazzle or alienate our gaze — they are neither cold, hard nor aggressive — but hold and deepen our attention until it crosses the threshold into another realm, in which the onus for constituting the aesthetic object has shifted from its own formal and self-contained parameters over into our own life-world; that is, into the realm of our own pure and concrete lived-experiences.

V.   SIGNALS/SILENCES

Barely three years after completing the *Webern* prints, Gaucher eschewed the diamond shape of the *Danse Carrées* in favor of the rectangle in a group of paintings that once again seem on first viewing to constitute a radical departure from what came before but which instead actually extend the thematic, conceptual and experiential reach of Gaucher's syntax as he develops his visual language. The *Danses Carrées* anticipate the horizontality characteristic of the *Signals/Silences*, through the inclusion of the linear element, the implied linear motif of small diamonds and the opening up of the linear compositions at right and left.

As Roald Nasgaard notes:

> The explicit diagonal will go "underground" for almost a decade in compositions at first organized entirely on horizontal and vertical relations. Implicitly, however, oblique vectors will continue to cross and recross almost all the paintings until the diagonal literally restates itself in *Deux Bruns, Deux Gris* in 1976.[35]

The titles of the new paintings include one or both of the terms "signals" or "silences," denoting the polarities, as Nasgaard further notes, on the one hand, of high colour contrasts and overt rhythmic schemas, and, on the other, of more subdued colour play instigating a mood of manifest reverence, a sort of contemplativeness, which will come to play an increasingly important role throughout Gaucher's subsequent painting, through the *Ragas* and *Grey on Grey Paintings*.[36]

The field is bracketed partially or in its totality by coloured edges which seemingly engage in a sort of "slow mime" of the linear elements within that bracketing, compressing them on the vertical axis. These "signals" are placed in what at first seem well-regulated tiers, or which suggest a hierarchy of interstices, one above the other, with an exhilirating sense of minute tonal and dispositional precision. The signals march in mathematically precise or dyadic, symmetrically-poised pairs in an almost incantatory rhythm down — or up, for that matter — the surface plane, a movement that seems as rigorous and uncompromising as it does unrelenting and inexorable. One might mistake the rhythm for a sort of threnody if there was not something so enlivening about it (see pl. 2).

One soon makes the uncanny connection with a Möbius strip, as if the "signals" were progressing on loops continuing under the base and round the top of the picture plane. The deliberative and distinctly "slow tempo" of the signals requires time for the full impact of the painting's field structure to propitiate itself. This may sound as though there is a real determinancy at work in these paintings. And there is — but only as long as they remain symmetrical. In the succeeding *Ragas*, as we shall see, executed hard on the heel of these works, things becomes progressively, even radically, more indeterminate in character. Always running parallel to advances in structuration is Gaucher's methodic complexifying of colour harmonics. His experiments in "pure" colour are readily discernible in the red, blue and yellow fields of many early *Signals/Silences*. With the painting called *Midnight Raga*, Gaucher started to consciously introduce harmonics into his colours, although arguably the later *Signals/Silences* demonstrate the first glimmerings of this methodology. Gaucher's concern for harmonics had its inception during the mixing of inks in his printmaking, specifically in creating different impressions of blacks through adding other colours. When, in painting, he started to mix his colours, he was pursuing the lessons learned in etching. The resultant harmonics are what lend his paintings their ineffable spectra of emotional tonalities, slowish temporality, and spiritual resonance.

These works are thus "quieter" than the preceding works, in which the lively and even eroticized kineticism has been toned down and there is more of a deliberate serenity in the rhythmic movements. But they are no less sensuous for all that. Nasgaard has understood this:

> A most palpable sensuousness is further suggested by the illusion which plays on the surface because of the relative location of colours in space, vibration of boundaries between contrasting hues of similar light intensity, or other effects brought about by the interaction of colour. The immaterial space thus created for vision becomes the proper arena for perceptual, imaginative and contemplative exploration.[37]

This "immaterial space" is so extraordinarily and distinctly Gaucher's own that it requires further clarification here. In the current paintings, as we shall see later, Gaucher has carried this immaterial space to its highest pitch thus far by pushing it further and, in the process, positing a virtual "dematerialization" of space across the breadth of the surface plane — a space that literally seems to be dematerializing as we observe it over time, as though it were really lifting off the phenomenal surface field and being indelibly impressed somewhere on the inside of our eyelids.

This haunting spatiality is, in its very methodical immateriality, then, one that confounds our attempts at pure description, and renders the temporality of our experience of a painting a place of palpable magic wherein colour reigns supreme and light holds sway.

VI. RAGAS, TRANSITIONS, GREY ON GREY PAINTINGS

Ragas

In the Ragas of 1967, as earlier noted, Gaucher made a bid for greater compositional freedom and considerably less constraint than was the case in the *Signal/Silences* that immediately precede them. This new series was characterized by the presence of a more pronounced intuitive ethic than was the case in the *Signal/Silences*. Once again, in this series as in other series in Gaucher's oeuvre, it was facilitated by a single work which advanced beyond the formal innovations of preceding work and showed a way of working forwards. The work in question this time was a silkscreen print produced near the end of 1966 entitled *XIV-9-66*. Arguably, the *Ragas* took a structural cue from the freer composition of this print. *Raga* itself refers to Indian music and François-Marc Gagnon has astutely pointed out that "in the *raga*, the monotone background played on the tanpura could correspond to Webern's silences."[38]

The *Ragas* are less "forthright" than their precursors, by which I mean they speak in gentler and lower, though no less eloquent, voices, lulling the observer into a more contemplative realm of the imagination. The rhythmic movements are more subliminal, and the paintings require more observation-time to fully assimilate and make sense of those movements. Gaucher returns to the syntax of the asymmetric in these paintings, but in a very low-profile way. And, by removing the bracketing devices characteristic of many of the *Signals/Silences* paintings, he is also, metaphorically, removing the barriers to the imaginative propensities of the observer achieving full play as the gaze is allowed to wander leisurely and at will through these phenomenally slow and seductive fields. This serves to break the physicality of the painting so that it transcends its objectival status. Throughout the *Signals/Silences*, and particularly in the last paintings in this series like *Signals # 2*, Gaucher was seeking to control and understand the behaviour and dynamism of the surface, expanding, compressing and distending various horizontal and vertical zones beyond the actual physical borders of the painting plane. In the *Ragas*, he was for the first time able to place a totalizing emphasis on non-physicality, opening up the field altogether and creating a contemplative spatiality, a magnetic lure for the imagination of the observer.

In *Cardinal Raga* (pl. 7), the majestic red field is like an imaginal framework through which the signals flow like melodic lines in a mantra slowly repeated; a resplendent and deeply calm surface which succours not only contemplation but motor atmosphere.

Plate 7   *Cardinal Raga*   1967

The *Transitions* suite of prints was a landmark work in that the individual prints dynamically bridge different series and transcend altogether what is often thought of as the secondary status of printworks in an artist's oeuvre. Indeed, Gaucher's prints must count, *en toto*, as one of the richest, most rigorous and sustained experiments in printmaking ever undertaken by a contemporary artist. Like the *Weberns*, these works become something more than simply prints. In any case, it is seldom that lithographs achieve such an exalted status and it is, unfortunately, a foregone conclusion that we will surely fail here in trying to convey to the reader either their import or their impact. They really have to be seen in themselves, preferably over a protracted time-span, such is their resilient strength and consummate subtlety.

As Nasgaard has noted, the first print in the portfolio has the identical organization of *Signals and Silences*, 1966, and the last projects into the *Grey on Grey Paintings*.[39] These prints are remarkable in their methodical and phenomenological exploration of myriad grey tonalities. Gaucher conceived this set of lithographs in 1967. Following preliminary drawings executed in the summer and fall of 1967, Gaucher spent months with the printer in Montreal collaborating on them, pushing the medium to the very limits of what was possible.

Thematically, the set demonstrates an extraordinary cohesiveness. The horizontal lines — Gaucher's signature "signals" — are dispersed with phenomenal exactitude across an open field. The rigorous and tellingly "reductivist" impulse that has always been implicit in the work prevails again here. The signals are sparse, more than "minimal" in degree and dispositional subtlety, dimension and placement. But the effect for the observer is far from minimal, even if it is one that requires, for full resolution, the utmost concentration, an attending akin to a sort of mental cupping of the ear, so that the ghostly rhythmic melodies inherent in each print can be made out above the distracting tumult that seems to pervade everything outside them. Indeed, the intonations are so faint and the harmonies so imperceptible to the eye that they can be reasonably likened to the barely perceptible overtones in instrumental music. Colour is limited to six light tonalities from black to the palest grey imaginable. It stands, as Doris Shadbolt has pointed out, as "a spectacular achievement in the medium."[40] Each line achieves its own transcendent, tensile and irreducible sense of selfhood on the basis of its precise definition in space, size and weight. As Shadbolt notes:

The character of the whole is one of clarity, stringency and a contained radiant energy. But the folio is not simply a collection of variations on a theme. The variations constitute a progression from one to eight so that each print is also grasped as part of a sequence. The final print is reached with a sense of excitement and arrival. The folio "is" the work and an aspect of the meaning of each print is its place in the whole.[41]

I have been fortunate in having had the opportunity to study the *Transitions* prints at some length and perhaps their most striking feature is the way they yield themselves so slowly to our perception, first, and subsequently to our understanding. It is not incidental to note that Gaucher executed these prints — but this is perhaps also true of all his other work — so they would be absolutely "unreproduceable," as he puts it. Even framing, however unobtrusive, introduces distracting elements. Certainly, any mechanical reproduction, of however high a quality, could never do full justice to them. A direct consequence of this is their exclusion from reproduction in this study. This is a tribute to their consummate subtlety.

Looking through them in their given order, one apprehends not only their phenomenological integrity but the perceptual and conceptual logic of the whole series, the sense of a slow and inexorable rhythm of life and unity, and a grasping of what was and is still perhaps destined to remain ineffable, in the sense of a litany of fragmented objectivities, all progressively moving towards autonomy and transcendence of the very concept that enabled them to be; towards, indeed, total freedom.

While the earliest works are seemingly predicated on given organizational laws, each succeeding print departs more and more from any pre-set organizational principles. One might suggest they become increasingly chaotic in that peculiar sense in which Gaucher tends to equate chaos with asymmetry. The "chaotic dynamics" at work here, however, does nothing to eclipse the phenomenal clarity and deep, even immeasurable, logic of the prints, particularly the last ones in the portfolio, but constitutes, in fact, their very foundation. For Gaucher there is nothing negative whatsoever about "chaotic dynamics" which is not about principles of randomness but a profoundly exacting methodology that affords new definitions of order that are simply incommensurable.

Plate 8   *V-I My-68*   1968

Grey on Grey Paintings

For the critic, the *Grey on Grey Paintings* present a real challenge and one that must be met with more than alacrity, because they demonstrate and demand the virtues of a purely presuppositionless description and the necessity for revising one's own schemas of interpretation in the process of perceiving. This is hard work. But then, the paintings require looking *hard*. In discussing this work, one can only ensure that as few presuppositions as possible remain to contaminate our reading strategies. Hence the need for a return to actual experience.

The *Grey on Grey Paintings* have been generally recognized as numbering among Gaucher's finest series to this date and, in fact, one of the stellar achievements in the history of Canadian painting (or international painting, for that matter). Any superficial reading of these paintings would render them somewhat less than daunting — so incredibly minimal and subtle are they — and absolutely fail in understanding them or be true to the experience of them. These paintings were not made for "rapid scanning." At first they seem mammoth, mercurial, even unfathomable grey fields, with extremely narrow linear elements of varying lengths floating on or emerging from their subtly-inflected surfaces. But in concentrated and protracted acts of observing, they become rather more than daunting. They become, in effect, breathtakingly alive.

The longer we prolong our confrontation with one of these paintings, say *V-I My-68* of 1968 (pl. 8), or *CB-I Mi-Je/69* (pl. 9) the more the ethereal grey field seems to hover overwhelmingly wraith-like before us, radiating a deep but expectant calm. Gradually, as our eyes are encouraged by the very stillness of the field to begin searching inquiringly within it, we seize upon short, horizontal, linear striations which seem to emerge abruptly from the field and then seemingly recede into it like apparitions, as we grow aware that other, narrower lines have emerged in their turn. Again, the primacy of Gaucher's "space duration" suggests itself; the fact that the observer, in and over time, constitutes the painting, drawing out its phenomenal latent content the longer one attends to it.

An unnatural stillness is offset by the sense of the field literally watching oneself. This gives way, by swiftly accelerating intervals, to our awareness that there is a phenomenal interplay between materializing lines that seemed truncated, arrhythmic and spectral only moments before, but now suddenly taut, rhythmic, and, in tandem, forming a sort of *coda* or, better yet, a *continuo* (as in music) for our ongoing perceptual apprehension of the work as a formal unity, anchoring its rhythmic melodies in the hidden harmonic base they effortlessly rise above. And the grey starts to cast off its mute greyness, yielding to another hue so much more seductive and nuanced that we wonder how we could have mistaken "mere" grey for this marvellous, seemingly unprecedented colour. The specifically hypnotic aspect of the *Grey Paintings* is largely owing to the perceived transformation of the simple grey field into a living entity that seems to slowly, almost imperceptibly, contract and expand, positing its own truth in the perceiving, composing its own rhythms — or is it *us* who compose them in the seeing? — and achieving its own sense of beingness in the very temporality of that seeing.

British curator and critic Bryan Robertson has recognized this, writing in *The London Spectator* (August 23, 1968), where he offers a wonderfully lucid, purely descriptive account of his encounter with the *Grey on Grey Paintings*:

> Imagine three very large, plain, grey paintings; the biggest, in the centre, some nine feet square, the two flanking canvases both seven feet by ten. Although the paintings are well spaced, an immediate impression of a somewhat solemn alignment has to be discounted: we are not confronted by a triptych with religious or hierarchical undertones. Three separate paintings face us in physical isolation; their only links being juxtaposition, similarity in shape, and the severity of their common greyness, which is dense and unbroken right across each surface. You see them with maximum objectivity in the prosaic, somewhat cold, but accurate conditions of plain daylight, modified and slightly softened by a muslin ceiling built across the top windows of the room, so that the paintings hang in a faintly underwater glow of cool and even light. After a while, it is clear that the three paintings are all of slightly different colour: the grey adjusts itself as the eye becomes conditioned and the painting on the left is revealed as a warm rose-grey; the central square painting a wholly neutral, untinted french or dove grey and a fraction lighter than the warmer painting to its left or the colder, slightly greenish-grey canvas to its right. All three are enlivened by sparse pale lines, of varying lengths, but all, evenly, about half an inch thick. The final discovery is that there are correspondences between the lengths of the lines at the top and base, for example, or at the sides, of the paintings. Coming to life and presenting highly intriguing puzzles to the eye the longer you

Plate 9   *CB-I Mi-Je/69*   1969

stare at them, these paintings yield the basic information outlined here in just about the same period of time as it has taken you to read so far. There are no side-tracks: the surfaces are even and anonymous, the grain of the canvas is concealed and, if there's no staining, there's no impasto either. The surface is like coloured Whatman paper. It is at this stage, when the eye really begins to work, to probe the secrets of these muted and powerfully restrained paintings — for they give out a sense of imminent revelation and of withholding, tantalizingly near the surface, mysterious insights into some new and unforeseen record of human activity — it is now that the paintings begin to take over the reflexes of the imagination as well as the eye.[42]

I have quoted this passage at some length because I believe its author is one of the few commentators to have apprehended with admirable clarity the phenomenological purity and meditative beauty of the *Grey on Grey Paintings* — and the fact that they seduce not only the eye but the imagination as well.

It is worth noting, I think, that the titles of the first *Grey on Grey Paintings* were simply *Alap*, referring to the arrhythmic, random and improvisatory sequences in an Indian *raga*, before the drumming begins and the rhythmic progressions start to assert themselves. The final series title is perhaps a tribute to the magnificent hegemony — and, for that matter, the heterogeniety — of chameleon greys in these canvases.

VI.   THE COLOUR BANDS

In 1971, Gaucher made another breakthrough with the *Colour Band* series. Various commentators have felt compelled to point out that he entered territory with this series that had already been staked out by other hard-edge colour-field painters. In fact, this sort of unfortunate comparison conceals the fact that the formal problems broached in this series were entirely fitting and salutary within the history of his own work and required the artist's sustained investigation at this particular juncture in his oeuvre.

It is neither reasonable nor germane to dwell on such comparisons when the internal logic of an oeuvre clearly anticipates certain developments which, for all their apparent relation to contemporaneous work being carried on outside that oeuvre, are absolutely necessary and even inevitable within it. If we study the logic of structural elements, specifically, linear elements from the *Signals/Silences* through the *Grey on Greys*, paintings with lines that gradually lengthen and become more and more resolved structurally and colouristically across the whole plane, we can see clearly that the evolutionary movement of line into band is inevitable and auspicious at this juncture within the still-ongoing formal development and internal purposefulness of this artist's work.

Gaucher said apropos the period just before the series was begun (he had recently executed the anomalous painting entitled *R-69*, which I will discuss shortly):

> I realized that it wasn't the philosophies that had to be short-circuited. It took me long to realize that, but it was the whole problem that had to be turned around to get another challenge.[43]

This painter does not forsake his "philosophies" in the *Colour Band* paintings, however radical a departure they may at first seem. As we look ever longer and harder, we realize that they do not constitute such a radical departure, after all, but instead represent a deepening and intensifying of the very core-thematics he habitually treated. It should be noted here that Gaucher's working methodology is really based on approaching formal matters in painting as "problems" that must be solved in practice. I would also hazard that while some commentators seem to feel that Gaucher dispensed entirely with the so-called "elusiveness" that characterized preceding work (the fact that a given painting in its entirety was constituted only over an inordinately long time span in the observing), these works, while proferring themselves in a fashion to be swallowed whole, as it were, take rather longer to digest than some have perhaps been willing to admit. The sheer weight of different

Plate 10   *Brun · Rouge · Orange/Ochre, Jaune et Vert*   1975

chromatic quanta achieves manifestation only over real time, as the colours are allowed to express their own essential features and specific individual masses within the overall composition, and their so-called "essences" longer still, as we slowly intuit the integrity of all horizontal territories, and those horizons given only in tandem, within the painting plane, shaped by Gaucher's exquisite and extraordinarily deft sense of measure.

Dore Ashton, in her 1975 article entitled "Yves Gaucher at the New York Cultural Center," has discussed what she calls her own "very subjective," but amazingly accurate and sensitive response to these paintings as follows:

> . . . Gaucher is concerned with weights and measures, and that is true in the enormous recent paintings so richly comparisoned in primary and earth colours. He weighs out so much earth-red brown, and so much afternoon blue, and so much sunflower yellow. Their interaction is not, however, preordained and here is where the deviation from the basic law distinguishes him. These colours are born only in concert, and would not exist without Gaucher's sense of measure. He measures shape, he measures intensity, he measures weight and *voila* a single impression, a singular impression. I daresay there are many for whom colour in itself means little. But I am among the others. Colour in itself elates me, and colour modulated by a passionate painter elates me especially. In his recent paintings, Gaucher announces clearly his own excitement given an abundance of colour. But that isn't all. Gaucher's colour, particularly in the largest canvases, works in various ways, and one of the ways is — there is no other way to say it — metaphorical. For informing the huge bands of differing colour, Gaucher has stretched them from boundary to boundary in an expression of powerful horizontal expanse. The energies of the hues here are distinctly felt moving rapidly, with coursing power, across successive horizons.[44]

As Ashton astutely notes, Gaucher's colours induce a curious elation, and we find ourselves thinking of associations with his progressions in nature, in music, in dance, in the very fabric of our lived-experience in the world. But the colours somehow escape those ideological values that inflect so much abstract painting and which would only vitiate them. In a painting like *Brun - Rouge - Orange/Ochre, Jaune et Vert* of 1975 (pl. 10), we are struck first, and we are left at last, with the palpable and exceedingly pure pleasure of colour itself.

For the painter's part, the effecting of colour-schemas that could give rise to such sheer exhiliration on his viewers' part was possible only because of his capacity to complexify the formal problems of the colour-field. This process of inquiry was empowered by the painting entitled *R-69*, a 9 x 15 foot Dayglo red painting that Gaucher contributed to the 1970 exhibition *Grands Formats* at the Musée d'art contemporain in Montreal. Gaucher has always been fearless when it comes to executing such bold and abrupt ruptures (not that many of them are allowed to see the light of day); ruptures which entail a shaking-up of the very foundations for his art, and a reassessment of prevailing directions, but never, however, an uprooting of its implicit philosophies.

I suspect that when Gaucher feels that something may be about to become theoretical, that is, when it threatens to become formulaic, he executes a painting that allows him some breathing-space and the promise of a new beginning. *R-69* was such a painting. (Not long ago, I saw another such radical painting in his studio which immediately predated the current *Pale Paintings* and very dramatically shortcircuited the sensibility of the *Dark Paintings* which preceded them.)

Virtual anomalies like *R-69* seem to represent a necessary and periodic purgation of Gaucher's more expressive propensities. Such an abrupt about-face has always had amelioratory ramifications for the work. *R-69* jettisons what we have come to believe are the characterizing stylistic insignias of this artist's work in order to open up not only new avenues for producing paintings but new ways of *thinking* painting. The radical form of self-questioning that a painting like *R-69* embodies is precisely what allows Gaucher to husband and perpetuate what many commentators have recognized as the inordinate formal purity of his "style." For anyone who familiarizes himself with Gaucher's oeuvre through leafing through a book of reproductions, it may not be immediately clear that such radical and discontinuous strategies in fact facilitate the underlying thematic continuity of this whole body of work.

Champ Vert (pl. 11) of 1971 is as much a true watershed in the development of Gaucher's oeuvre as *R-69* was a radically discontinuous one that allowed him to short-circuit the threat of eventual formal theorization. Gaucher is always looking ahead, assessing what look like promising directions and what might well foretell dead-ends. Certainly, and by any standard, the work in question must count as a significant breakthrough. The painting is comprised of a minimal field of greenish-grey crossed by four asymmetrically positioned horizontal white lines. The centre line seems marked by a slightly more declarative value of white than the others. The lines demarcate the overall field into

Plate 11   *Champ Vert*   1971

five highly individualised zones or bands, tautening out the elasticity of the horizonal structure — in the phenomenological sense of a pre-delineated zone of possibilities — and horizontal slant of the surface plane. The respective values of these bands seemingly undergo subtle and minute changes the longer we look at them. But these changes are so subtle that we are left with considerable uncertainty as to the scope, intensity or time-factor of the change. Our knowledge of that uncertainty clues us in to the phenomenological, spatial and temporal flux implicit in the painting; we are aware of its "beauty" but we are also aware of its behavioural cast and the fact that it changes the longer we contemplate it. This painting still has something of the sprit of the *Grey on Greys* but directly foretells the emergence of the *Colour Bands*.

As Nasgaard has noted, the works dating from 1971 and 1972 integrated into the single canvas "both the effect of play between several hues and the rhythmic movement of the network of signals."[45] Each painting has two entirely separate horizontal systems of bands. One order is delineated by the different tonalities of grey and the other is delineated by the white lines. The edges between the colour bands, as Nasgaard further notes, evade "precise definition in vision and seem to hover somewhere not quite on the surface of the painting."[46] This is correct. By steady gradations, the number of horizontal white lines lessens from four to one, as, for instance, in *Blue, Purple and Green* of 1972. In the course of 1972 the lighter greys are eschewed in favor of browns, blues and darker greys. In early 1973, the white lines are completely forsaken, and the horizonal structure is delimited to horizontal colour bands of diverse widths and number.

The *Colour Bands* as a series are largely concerned with the dynamics of pure color and do perhaps yield a far more confrontational, even "brutal" interface, as some have claimed, with the optic than was the case with the preceding series. This is certainly true of the work in the Mackenzie Gallery collection, *Bruns, Jaune et Rouge* (pl. 1) dating from 1973, the first and one of the most important of the *Colour Bands* and which is deserving of special commentary here. It immediately precedes the painting of the same title which appears and is discussed at some length in the catalogue for the 1979 exhibition at the Art Gallery of Ontario *Yves Gaucher: A Fifteen-Year Perspective, 1963-1978*. Nasgaard's discussion of the other *Bruns, Jaune et Rouge* is telling and bears repeating here:

> It is divided bluntly, and with a certain abruptness, into four ascending bands of colour; brown, red, yellow and brown. The browns are matte, heavy and inert. One pushes upwards

ponderously from below, the other, although the narrowest, presses downwards from above with the weight of lead. The two squeeze out between them the yellow and red which, because they are bright and expansive, can only regain their necessary space by pushing out towards the spectator. If Albers has spoken of a painting "looking at us," then the *Bruns, Jaune et Rouge* is a case of a painting squaring its shoulders and baring its chest ready for battle.[47]

When I refer to the painting that Nasgaard discusses as "the other" *Bruns, Jaune et Rouge*, it is important to note that the painting in the Mackenzie collection is a slightly smaller but otherwise very similar version of this same painting. However, it predates it and, as a matter of fact, is thus historically the first in which the graphic element disappears altogether and is replaced by the band. This helps explain, perhaps, why two versions were executed. Gaucher recognized its import immediately. He has said that he views this work as one of the major paintings in his whole oeuvre and reprised it precisely because the shift from graphic element to band was a "major stretch." It is also "the first painting to deal directly with colour."[48] In fact, it is the first to move beyond the syntax of the *Grey on Greys* into the realm of what we might call "heavy colour."

But, while the two paintings in question are extremely alike, compositionally speaking, the actual self-presence of the colours, while otherwise close in value, differ rather markedly. The yellow in the Mackenzie collection painting seems so bold and forthright that it has nothing of the more sullen cast of the work that Nasgaard discusses. It is a brilliant yellow that eludes or blunts the pincers of the surrounding brown and red. It seems to emanate outwards, over the head of the observer, like the brilliant light that rhythmically flushes out of the eerie slit in the head of a sci-fi Robby-the-Robot. It also seems to buoy up the whole composition, as if investing its heavy mass with an antigravitational force. The yellow is hence the linchpin of the dynamic equilibria of the whole composition and anchors it in our perception in a life-enhancing, rather than a purely aggressive or limiting, way. Reproductions do not do full justice to this yellow but the greatest care has been taken to ensure that the plate in this book is at least halfway suggestive of its real integrity. It should be noted that between these two works (both versions of *Bruns, Jaune et Rouge*, 1973) and *Orange, Jaune et Ochres, Ieire Version* (1974), Gaucher executed some symmetrical paintings. Gaucher returned to symmetry once again in order to define the very parameters of a problem he desired to solve. In other words, as he

Plate 12 *Deux Bruns, Deux Gris* 1976

puts it, "I had not only to verify once again what the principles were but fathom and control them in order to break them."[49]

Several commentators have pointed out that the visual experience of these *Colour Band* paintings is utterly distinct from the preceding works, particularly the *Grey on Grey* series. Again, the fact remains that, as the reader will have understood by now, each of the foregoing series was a different experience in its own right, as witness, for instance, our discussion of the *Danses Carrées*. Each series that Gaucher creates is executed for different reasons, to address different problems, to afford the observer different experiences. It is hard to understand, then, why these paintings should seem to some as such an abrupt departure. Each series, in fact, marks a departure. But all challenge our perception. All, however stylistically disparate they may seem, manage to transcend their own physicality in affording us an experience that is existential and even exalting. Thus, the underlying *telos* or thematic and purposive reach of the work is always preserved intact and stengthens as it progresses, even if, in the *Colour Bands*, the problem of colour is addressed far more directly, empirically, and in a somewhat different way than in preceding series.

It is interesting to note that it was necessary for Gaucher to "tune" many of these paintings by modulating, and often by the barest increments of tonal change, one or more of its colours. As Nasgaard notes, because this artist uses primed canvases, such adjustments are not as arduous as they are for stain painters who must succeed on the very first try or dispense with the canvas.[50] Yet his exquisite precision and assuredness is the hard-won product of years' practice in structuring a painting. In the years before 1970 Gaucher used working drawings but in the series after 1970, when structure and colour became phenomenally intertwined, drawings were used only as a vehicle for exploring new ideas as opposed to preliminary sketches for prospective paintings.

Gaucher has said:

> The physicality of working a big painting, and the scale, is very different for a smaller one. I like to bounce between the big and the small, on the same premise basically, just to reassess where the problem is. Sometimes you get carried away with a very large painting and you try to convince yourself that it is working. But as soon as you bring the problem back to the small one you sense that there is something wrong which you have to settle in the small one before going back to the big one, or vice-versa. To work on more than one painting refreshes my head and forces me to keep it open in more than one direction.[51]

Nasgaard has noted that a painting's development through multiple stages, which may yield as many as five paintings different in both structure and colour, is explicitly concerned with colour weights and measures. Yet, if the colours in question are always articulated in beguiling concert, it is still true, I think, that the individuality of each should not be deprecated and, while Nasgaard has maintained that Gaucher is not interested in colour presentation or colour definition in itself (i.e. with putting the emphasis on their individuality or on their differences), an intimate knowledge of that individuality is nonetheless necessary in order to judge how they will interact in concert and, in fact, it is something of a truism that their individuality must be sufficient to preserve their integrity if the phenomenal field in which they are situated is to be finally understood as a formal unity.[52]

Gaucher methodically explores the phenomenal tensions between various colours, weighing out value, hue and chroma judiciously so as to successfully impart the character of specific experiences. And the paintings themselves may fittingly be read as sequences of "breathing apertures," each colour-band akin to a breath deeply inhaled, so deeply, indeed, that we think for a moment it will not be exhaled, until we grasp the painting once again as an expansive unity. Then, as our gaze apprehends the bands as individuals, the painting begins to draw in its breath again. Each deep "inhalation" and "exhalation" throws silent ripples not only across the surface of this rhythmic domain, but across the surface of our reflection.

And it should be pointed out that Gaucher's methodology certainly distinguishes him from colour-field painters like the well-known American Kenneth Noland (although certain similarities with other colour-field painting will be discussed presently). Nasgaard has astutely noted salient differences between the two painters:

> Gaucher's emphatic exploitation of the tensions between colours, and between them and their structural container, also distinguishes him from Noland, who is more concerned with the immediate character of colours and with exploring their relations in harmonious sequences. In his horizontal stripe paintings Noland has also, on the whole, avoided extremes of saturation in his hues, especially in the broader bands. He has tended to separate his bands with narrow strips of raw canvas to ease colour transitions.[53]

More important, however, is the fact that Gaucher does not flirt with the now rather dated strategies of optical dazzle or illusionism, which Noland has had recourse to throughout much of his career.

It should be stressed that, while he does posit in the *Colour Bands* a painting as a pictorial unity that must be grasped at once, if one digested over time, it does not necessarily entail a *non-contemplativensss* in the seeing. Form may become secondary to brute colour, and asymmetry may be a methodologically liberating ploy, but the tension and release associated with colours and their motor atmosphere are profoundly implicated in the perception of the *Colour Bands*. They are especially interesting in that the gaze grounds them in their unity by palpating, in its traversal, the bands like folds in the phenomenal field, familiarizing itself with tension-dynamics, and then giving itself over completely to the wider rhythmic harmony of the work. As well, very few of the *Colour Band* paintings are symmetrical. These paintings stake a compelling claim on the faculties of the observer and, if the attempt to synthesize any one painting colour band by colour band fails because it is apprehended as a unitary, if asymmetrical, structure first and foremost, it is still true that it is constituted in its individual parts and their interrelationships over time.

While it may seem that Gaucher has radically changed the parameters of his working methodology in this series, choosing horizontality over verticality to invoke the real phenomemon of weight and to undermine the logic of linear reading strategies, he has in fact remained true to his own first, best destiny: turning the tables on himself in order to push forward his formal language and not forsaking those implicit philosophies which lend continuing impetus to all his work. In bringing into play the dynamism of vertical relationships between the colour bands, and in the process formulating a system of dynamic tensions in both directions (and placing equal pressure on all peripheries of the picture plane), Gaucher rules out sequential reading strategies in favor of thematic holistic reading and "reading by weight and measure" (this latter is itself a formidable advance and one not adequately recognized as such).

In the paintings of 1974-75 Gaucher is preoccupied with horizontal and vertical orientations in field-structure. The diagonal sometimes appears, presaging the later *Jerichos*. The totalizing asymmetrical structure of the band paintings of 1976 enabled Gaucher to progressively reinstate the diagonal as a methodological and stylistic device, as he finally did in *Deux Bruns, Deux Gris*, 1976 (pl. 12). It is important to note that a decade after executing the painting in the Mackenzie collection, *Signals #2* (pl. 2), he produced this important painting, which himself says grew directly out of it. Certainly, the colour-schemas of the two paintings are remarkably similar. This is not unusual for Gaucher, since a hallmark of his work is periodically reinstituting interesting, if unresolved or unexhausted, colour and related problems and concerns in order to take a fresh perspective upon them, so that they acquire a new resonance and a new promise in the present. This painting is also important in that it sets the stage for the later *Jerichos*, which have similar colour schemas, specifically the first two in the series. It also presages the unilaterally dark values of the more recent *Dark Paintings*. *Deux Bruns, Deux Gris* has an entirely asymmetrical arrangement of three horizontal bands but the one in the center is complicated by a diagonal which divides it, also asymmetrically, and thus forces the *Colour Bands* beyond their original parameters into the more totalizing asymmetry of his *Jerichos*.

Plate 14   *SF, 3-86*   1986

Plate 15 *Br Bl. Rd.*   1984

VIII. THE JERICHOS, WORKS ON PAPER, SQUARE PAINTINGS, DARK PAINTINGS

In the series called *Jerichos*, begun in 1976, Gaucher confronted directly the problem of the diagonal and so fulfilled the implicit promise of asymmetry as a latent formal and methodological principle in his entire corpus. Thus, some fourteen years after the *Webern* prints, he explicitly tackled asymmetrical diagonal compositional structures that had been on-again, off-again thematic and stylistic facets of his work in the interim. He subtitled many of the paintings "An Allusion to Barnett Newman." But, as Nasgaard has noted, the term "allusion" should be understood in the widest possible sense.[54] Emphatically, it is just an allusion, and is not indicative of an ideological alliance or an appropriation. Gaucher was obviously struck by Newman's *Jericho* painting but had seen it only through the medium of black and white reproduction. He had not seen the original. Indeed, it was not important for him to see the original. Perhaps because he was intuitively struck by the implicit promise of the structural character of the painting in question, the diagonal/triangle, for the logic of his work's development at this time. Certainly, he recognized certain affinities between Newman's endeavour and his own concerning the complex problem of asymmetry. It is worth quoting Nasgaard, I think, with respect to the salient intentional and methodological differences between Newman and Gaucher despite the superficial stylistic likenesses:

> If Newman understood the triangle as a truncated rectangle, Gaucher put it back inside the rectangle. Where Newman bisected his black ground with a narrow band of red, Gaucher cut the rectangular plane down the middle, creating a diptych format. He separated the two canvases just enough to establish the necessary tension between the triangular sections in each half of the diptych.[55]

Gaucher radically maximizes a marginal asymmetry in Newman's canvasses, by shunting the truncated triangle further off axis so that its halves are unequal in area, angled differently and entirely distinct in characteristic spirit.

These paintings are rife with paradoxes for perception. They also demonstrate a phenomenal cohesion whereby one zone, considered in itself, soon snaps into place with the suddeness of a steel trap within our perception of the surface plane, so that the whole composition is dramatically united in a single traversal of the gaze. In that very moment, the observer is apt to experience something akin to awe, and his somatic pact with the painting is sealed.

Gaucher has often been quoted as saying that in his use of a large scale it is never "big for bigness' sake"; that the "content" of his paintings requires an inordinately large scale. This is especially true for the *Jerichos*, with their huge truncated triangles that address the whole body sensibility of the observer in an immediate way. Unfailingly, they attain a perfect pitch of proportion, exquisite rightness of dimension, and exemplary overall field-structure. Such is the case in the painting entitled *Jericho 2* of 1978 (pl. 13).

From 1980 to 1983, Gaucher executed little painting and few prints because of health reasons. Sadly, it was just too taxing. However, this was a far from fallow period. The few works that he executed, including

Fig. 2   *Phases I, II, III*   1981

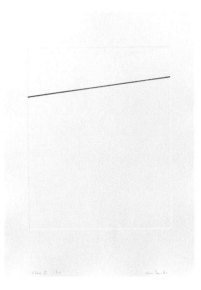

the two sets of prints called the *Phases* and *Inversions*, demonstrated some advances and some avenues for future investigation that he will probably be pursuing well into the 1990s.

Gaucher himself emphasizes the importance of the *Phases* series of three prints, entitled *Phase I, Phase II* and *Phase III* respectively (fig. 2).

The artist recognizes the crucial role these triptych, drypoint engravings on copper played in propelling him beyond the formal language of the *Jerichos*, the angles, tensions and preoccupation with shape of which at this point threatened to become static. In the *Phases*, Gaucher started dealing with a given area as a purely rhythmic element that had very little to do with form. While the line bisected the whole surface into two areas, it also set up a rhythmic interplay between two masses that had seemingly dematerialized. The line does not fix the contours of a shape but defines the space on both sides of itself, as it were. These prints are the distinct precursors of his current *Pale Paintings*, in which the demarcation between any two colours is used as a line that enhances the rhythmic movement of colour energies across the whole plane as they dematerialize, pushing out or receding into real, lived-space.

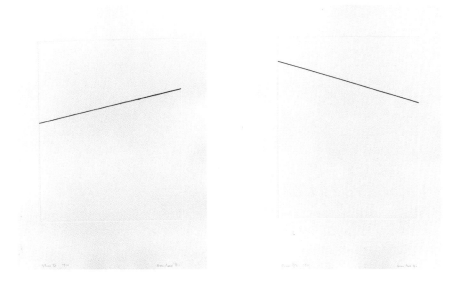

Gaucher exhibited a major group of works on paper at the Olga Korper Gallery in Toronto in 1986. Often in these works, Gaucher privileges only one or two of the diagonal zones with pure colour. They stand out with intense clarity against the white sheet of paper. In several curious, atypical works, felt-pen and wax are used within the diagonal configuration in a gestural way, the brushstroking taking on a primacy denied it in all the other work. In a few works, the diagonal cedes to cruciform configurations comprised of dramatically differentiated rectilinear blocks of pure unadulterated chroma crossed one over another, skewing the rectangles off their axes and heightening the overall sense of asymmetry. One can sense in these paper works a desire on the artist's part to push the formal language of the *Jericho* series ever further, even to the breaking-point, in order to tackle new problems and open up new possibilities. In *SF, 3-86* (pl. 14), Gaucher included a diagonal pencil line that is reminiscent of the line in the *Phases* prints, a diagonal pencilled zone with pencil stroking and eschewing linear definition at the right, with a further painted zone in colours, the contrast between the effects of different media itself yielding a staccato rhythm.

Co-extensively with the period of experimentation of the works on paper, Gaucher executed a series of works that would become known as the *Square Paintings*. These paintings were well-received when exhibited at Olga Korper Gallery in Toronto and are largely responsible, with their successors the *Dark Paintings*, for the renewed interest in Gaucher's work in recent years. Begun in 1983, these canvases at first seem to forsake the structural integrity of the *Jerichos*, but in fact develop it further, collapsing the horizonality of the *Jerichos* into the format of squares, and starting to deepen the hues unilaterally across the spectrum, presaging the rich, earthlike browns, magentas, greens and other darker values of his soon-to-emerge *Dark Paintings*. They give the effect of spatial layering like a receding series of veils. Planes succeed one another across the painting plane in a horizontal rhythmic movement established longtitudinally through a diagonal flux, as is the case in the painting called *Br Bl. Rd of 1984* (pl. 15). These works were first exhibited as a group in April 1985 at the Olga Korper Gallery in Toronto, and were seemingly anchored to the floor plane. The top line of each painting thus constituted a broken, but continuous line which pulled all the paintings together into a cohesive environmental statement. This methodology of installing works so as to create an environment (which I will discuss in more depth presently) was first realized in the exhibition of the *Grey on Grey Paintings* at the Vancouver Art Gallery in 1969. Doris Shadbolt was instrumental in affording Gaucher the opportunity to formulate this methodology by giving him great latitude in the hanging of the rooms at the Gallery. He came to realize as a result of that hanging, during which he created twin "cool" and "warm" rooms, that he could put together another statement, one greater than the sum of the individual paintings, at once an installation, an event, and a whole environment.

These works were then subsumed by the *Dark Paintings* proper. The seductive, autumnal colour-schema of a painting like *R-/R-Red* of 1988 (pl. 16) with its deep, rich earth hues conveying all the vitality of the soil, sap of the soul, is a glorious register of this artist's continuing search for rhythms as vital and dynamic as those in nature itself. Towards the latter half of the series, Gaucher once again stretched out the horizontal format and, when exhibited at Olga Korper, hung the paintings bare inches off the floor, ensuring maximum somatic impact on the observer by establishing a concrete relation between painting and body, the latter playing a major role in assimilating the work. The painting literally becomes a *situation* as opposed to a length of painted canvas; an *event* rather than an object.

IX.   THE PALE PAINTINGS: LIGHT AS CONTENT

The *Pale Paintings* were begun as recently as Summer, 1988. Consummation and breakthrough, they represent a radical synthesis of all the artist's antecedent concerns. While preserving, in the early works, the diagonal format that had prevailed since *Deux Bruns, Deux Gris*, they are also clearly related in colour-sensibility and slow tempo to the *Grey on Grey Paintings* and, recently, in this still-ongoing series, have moved altogether out of the shadow of the *Jerichos*.

There is a grey or pale zone or panel in each painting, which establishes the connection with the *Grey on Greys*. But, in this series, Gaucher pushes beyond anything he has achieved before in colouristic terms, for the specific colours in these paintings are unlike any other colours he has ever created. Gaucher himself has spoken of the significant influence of Claude Monet, particularly his waterlily canvasses, on the *Grey and Grey Paintings* and subsequent work. The emphasis is on non-physicality, and "a light from nowhere" as he puts it (see pls. 17, 18).[56]

Rosalind Krauss, in her important essay "On Frontality," has discussed Claude Monet's later work in connection with Modernist painters like Stella, Olitski and Poons. Her discussion is relevant here:

> Monet's vision of the dense floral pools which he constructed around him in monumental walls of paint was a vision which conflated three separately given objects of sight into a single interlace of pigment. In the long strokes of divided colour which coupled on the plane of the canvas, he conveyed the sky which he felt above him; the reeds and stems growing from the bottom of the ponds; and the physical support for both the lily pads and the sky's reflections, which was the surface of the pool itself. Lines of blue, white and green, lying close-knit on the plane of the canvas not only allowed one to focus on that plane but expanded it as well — wrenched it apart to include a deep and luminously refractive world.[57]

The experiential touchstone that the pond represented for Monet is somewhat akin to the experiential, "natural" sources for Gaucher's work, in which all the peculiar voluminosity of a "deep and luminously refractive" world is translated effortlessly into massive planes of colour and light that interact in hauntingly rhythmic ways. In his latest paintings, Gaucher has seemingly captured what Krauss calls the "internal expansion of every point of the picture's surface."[58] Colour and the literal plane of the picture are indissolubly wed. The current paintings seem to be lit from behind, suffused with a soft internalized light that irradiates throughout the surface plane yet nevertheless radiates outwards and encompasses the observer's intending perception, at the very wellsprings of desire and bodiliness. Light has truly become the one inalienable content of these paintings.

Gaucher himself acknowledges the "family resemblance" of the *Pale Paintings* to the *Grey on Greys* in terms of a fairly close sense of light, serenity and "softness," extended durational temporality and obtrusive spatiality. Both series have a very strong environmental quality. The *Pale Paintings* are hung low, affording the observer the nascent, if slightly unnerving, feeling that one is actually walking into the painting. At the same time, the painting seems to come out from the wall on which it is hung, meeting one half-way in the process, its frontality affording one full-purchase bodily.

Gaucher refers to his love for and indebtedness to the specific, if still virtually indescribable, quality of light in the paintings of 17th-Century Dutch painter Vermeer, as well as in certain works of Pieter de Hoogh and, to a lesser extent, Pieter Jansz Saenredam. In 1983, Gaucher travelled to Amsterdam, and spent many long hours in the Stedejlik Museum studying the work of the Dutch masters.

Vermeer, in paintings like his remarkable *View of Delft* (incidentally, a favorite of Gaucher's), achieved a genuine and sensuous intensity in developing colours which can only be called uniquely his own — for example, his signature blue, a blue as quintessentially Vermeer's as that other blue of the Arena Chapel frescoes was Giotto's — by virtue of fusing those colours with light so absolutely that the picture plane takes on an unearthly glow, as if lit from behind.

Albert Barnes has written perceptively on Vermeer:

> In the best of Vermeer, colour has, as in no other Dutch painter except Rembrandt, full structural significance, and drawing is a perfect merging of light, colour and line. Contours vary from an accentuated broad line to complete absence of line. The masses thus constructed are bound together by rich, rhythmic linear patterns, colour-relations, and pervasive light in compositions which are felt as coloured rhythmic sequences of volumes in deep space.[59]

The pervasive light in the *Pale Paintings* is enhanced by the impression that this light seems to emanate from somewhere behind the painting plane. But it is so phenomenally fused with Gaucher's new and almost uncategorizable colours — this moist verdigris, that smoky mauve — that they cannot be readily differentiated. Like the light in the best Vermeers he loves, it is quite impossible to draw any fine distinction between colour and light in Gaucher's latest paintings. The light is the colour and the colour is the light, and both seem, in a phrase, unerringly right. Furthermore, as our eyes sweep through the zones of light, the sense of a rhythmic sequencing is very strong, but it is one that stems more from the impression of the *passage of light* through the far reaches of an intuitively-generated space than it does from symphonic movements generated in the geometric space of hard-edge composition. The colour-relations are as haunting as they are indescribable, as zones and panels are juxtaposed in ways that should not work but which invariably work successfully.

The spatial anisotropy of any one painting is exceptionally strong, yet the viewer is encouraged less to sway along with the rhythmic schema than to attempt to secure it in memory or maintain the same station-point in space for a time in order to digest and contemplate it sufficiently. There is a sense in which the soft colours themselves seem to be lifting off the plane altogether like layers of pollen in a breeze; in their unearthly clarity, they seem to achieve frontality in real space, as opposed to being limited to a picture plane. This frontality serves the purpose of redeeming the painting from the structures of its physicality — thus fulfilling Gaucher's own latent intentionality, as discussed in Part One — by shifting it over wholesale into the viewer's own lived-space.

While light becomes the absolute content of the *Pale Paintings*, it is by no means a radical departure from foregoing series, for both the *Square Paintings*, with their shifting veils of colour/light and the *Dark Paintings*, in which lighter forms seem to be hovering like phantasms behind the darker zones, use light as content, even if it is therein more subliminal than overt. The problem of light reaches even further back in the corpus, of course, but in the later series of work we can sense it moving towards full resolution as thematic "content." The *Dark Paintings* and the current paintings demonstrate a maximal use of colour harmonics which allows full release of light.

Martin Pops has written eloquently of Vermeer's *Soldier and Laughing Girl*: "Thoré tells of a man who looked behind it in order to discover the source of its incandescence. Vermeer paints an innocent brightness, not the light of common day, even as he paints a space which, like the depth of an opaque vessel, still preserves its secrecy. This space is beyond sight and below time."[60] Similarly, we are puzzled as to the source of the light that suffuses one of the *Pale Paintings* and are almost driven to look behind the painting to see what that source could be. This secret light lies somewhere between words and silence, between a first light and the first tinges of twilight, and is shed as much on the eye that would experience it as on the mind and the imagination that would know it. It says much, I think, about Gaucher's very considerable achievement that we can only have recourse to remarks like Barnes' or Pops' apropos Vermeer to do justice to these pale, elusive but wholly engrossing paintings, with their atmospheric passages of pure light, either in purely descriptive accounts or as a testament to the specifically pleasurable quality of our perceptual experience of them.

Certain paintings in this series eschew the asymmetry of the diagonal altogether. But we cannot call them "striped" or "vertical band" paintings because the vertical divisions in the horizontal plane are so wide that they seem like huge, rectangular, but architecturally discrete, blocks seamlessly wed by the sonorities continually generated by colour-relationships across the whole plane. It is also worth noting that, while most of the paintings do include the diagonal, and the vertical, they are no longer structural features as such so much as purely rhythmic elements. For instance, in the latest (and largest) of the *Pale Paintings* (pl. 18), the diagonal on the far right serves the function of rebounding the rhythmic movement back upon itself, as in a closed loop, endlessly regenerating the pulsating rhythm that slowly moves across the whole surface, starting with the deep, mustard yellow through the orange and light green, barely penetrating the grey and then sent on its way back again to the far left. This remarkable painting must be counted as one of the most radical Gaucher has executed to date, with its colour-schemas and relationships that one feels should not work but which invariably do, and furthermore, which touch on some of the same colour choices as the *Danses Carrées* but which set up a situation in which coloured space dematerializes and light assumes a primacy it never had before, a situation that perhaps only a quarter century of intense experimentation and learning could yield.

The *Pale Paintings* return in a sense to the overtly phenomenological language of the *Grey on Grey Paintings* in being addressed to the perceptual experience of the observer above and beyond purely formal concerns. Our status as creative beings is foremost, and the lived-experience of the paintings is nothing short of enlivening. In this respect, they are like stirring spring sunshine after the deep fall of the *Dark Paintings*, providing a felt counterpoint to the latter's umbrage of hue and more sombre moods. Gaucher has here demonstrated his mastery of colour-harmonics (as distinct from chroma) and if light can be characterized as the subject-matter of these paintings it is precisely because of his meticulous play with the harmonics, which results in a wealth of emotional nuances and seductive tonalities.

M.E. Chevreul has said:

> All the primary colours gain in brilliancy and purity by the proximity of Grey; yet the effects are far from being similar or even analogous, to those which result from the proximity of the same colours with White. There is nothing surprising in this, when we consider that if White preserves to each colour its character, and even heightens it by contrast, it can never itself be taken for a colour properly so called; as Grey, on the contrary, can be so, it happens that it produces with the darkest colours — such as Blue, Violet, and the deep tones in general — assortments which enter into analogous harmonies; whilst, with colours naturally brilliant — such as Red, Orange, Yellow, and the light tones of Green — they form harmonies of contrast. Now, although White contrasts more with the sombre colours than with those that are naturally luminous, we cannot observe between White and these two classes of colours the difference which we distinguish between Grey and these same colours.[61]

The foregoing remarks might be said to constitute something of the "theory" behind the *Pale Paintings* with their myriad delicate nuances and interrelations of grey with other colours, if it were not for the fact Gaucher discovered these principles in the practice, rather than importing them through the theory and if it were not for the fact that Gaucher effectively *inverts* Chevreul's thesis. Hence, the above remarks fail to fully establish the empirical validity of the specific tonal interplay in Gaucher's current paintings. The colours in a given canvas do not gain in brilliance through their proximity to grey, but change the "factual" reading of the grey to an "actual" hue, imbuing the grey with a manifest richness of modulations. It is also important to remember that Gaucher's use of grey — this "chameleon" colour, as he calls it — is career-long, from the *Weberns* through the current paintings. In the *Danse Carrées*, the *Signals/Silences*, and, of course, the *Grey on Greys*, grey was used frequently and even thematically. Indeed, grey is truly, and perhaps strangely (at least for those who have been sizably impressed with his other colours, as in the *Colour Bands*), his signature colour.

Now, whereas in the *Grey on Grey* paintings it was one subtly-inflected grey (never just 'grey' but a rose-grey in one painting, a violet-grey in the next and so forth) per surface field of any one painting, in the *Pale Paintings* the similarly-nuanced grey occupies only one determinate zone which interrelates with other zones, sometimes subtle and sometimes overt in their harmonic cadences and chromatic differences.

As each zone, grey or otherwise, "dematerializes," it seems to occupy a larger space than it in fact does but does not overlap or impinge on others, but seems to subtend them, yielding continually reorganized rhythmic schemata that move from right-to-left and left-to-right asymmetrically across the surface plane. The colours in closest proximity to the grey may seem at first to gain immeasurably in brilliance and purity accordingly, but the grey itself becomes subtly inflected by the spectra of those other colours, while simultaneously, if paradoxically, eluding any exact definition and thus frustrating any attempts at final taxonomy.

Berhard Kerber has written on the work of contemporary German abstract artist Dieter Jung in a way which seems to establish a certain parallel or kinship with Gaucher's endeavour:

> The materiality and surface texture of these spatial colour-veils are fashioned in such a way as to become irridescent in changing light; they are neither nebulous nor solid. Pigment loses its materiality; the immateriality of the material is revealed. The colours deny the viewer any certainty about their existence in the measure in which they fluidly change their spatial value time and again within the systematic texture of the painting. Presence and dissolution are the subjects here. Autonomous pictorial space and heteronomous viewer's space start to communicate. The picture loses its integral existence in contrast to the wall and a tendency towards environment becomes evident.[62]

While Gaucher's current paintings certainly become more than just physical fact (they become somehow *alive* in the viewing, and achieve the phenomenal similitude of *respiration* in the observing), he does not, as Jung does, forsake the clarity of his colours which, for all their immateriality and harmonic interplay, achieve a high effect of hallucinatory clarity. But the achievement of that clarity is all the more remarkable given that any one of these paintings becomes a manifestly *environmental* object.

I think there is far more justification in relating Gaucher's work to that of an iconoclastic figure like Jung than in relating it to the American colour-field painters, and this precisely because of Gaucher's own iconoclasm.

Yet, if there is any common ground to be found with the colour-field painters, it resides in the area of a shared visionary intention or, more properly perhaps, in visionary results. Certainly, Gaucher, like many of the leading colour-field painters, had the overt, if unstated, intention of making work that would be at once sublime and transcendent.

It was to Russian Constructivist Kazimir Malevich that he looked for inspiration, and it is worth noting that the problem of asymmetric structuration that Malevich opened up was one that he felt was worth exploring himself. But, as we have seen, his aim to create an expanse that would extend beyond the picture edges was akin to what the colour-field painters avowedly wanted in their work.

Gaucher himself adamantly opposes being assimilated into any group or school, and if he is something of a maverick, this has to do with his own search for personal identity. For Gaucher, identity only comes from looking methodically within, to the inner man, in order to realize the universal man. According to him, this is the only true source from whence a "national identity" can be said to stem.

Irving Sandler, in *The Triumph of American Painting: A History of Abstract Expressionism*, expressed best what establishes the kinship between the art of Gaucher and that of colour-field painting:

> The huge size of colour-field abstractions fulfilled [this] function: pictures that fill the viewer's field of vision become a kind of environment, special places that engage him with immediacy while screening him from his everyday surroundings and releasing him from them.[63]

Similarly, Gaucher works on a large scale in order to render the observer's field of vision a sort of holistic contemplative environment in which communing feelingly with the painting becomes a very real prospect and not just an empty, unfulfilled intention on the painter's part. As we have noted frequently thoughout this text, on its monumental scale the painting sets up a physical situation in which it becomes more than just a snare for the unwary optic. The experience of colour is then not merely visual. On this scale, it is a somatic experience. The body of the observer becomes crucial.

Certainly, in his current *Pale Paintings*, Gaucher has pushed his painting syntax to a new level of observer-involvement and in it he achieves a genuine synthesis of insights and formal breakthroughs culled from all preceding series, but particularly from the *Grey on Grey Paintings*, while demonstrating a whole new understanding of colour and light, and one which he has spent his entire creative lifetime working towards.

X. CONCLUSION: PAINTING AS COMMUNION AND ENVIRONMENTAL CONCEPT

Right from the very outset of his career as an artist, Gaucher sought something other than a mere theoretical or material statement in his work. According to the exigencies of his intuitive ethic, and his empirical methodology, he wanted to proffer the possibility of an experience that would extend beyond the actual dimensions of a given work, whether it be a *Webern*, a *Raga* or one of the current *Pale Paintings*, that is, some larger statement that would not stop at the physical limits of the painting plane but would stake a claim on the observer's own lived-space and subsequently secure that observer's physical and spiritual sympathy with it.

Gaucher has always been preoccupied with formulating an environment for vision, a framework for *seeing* and *feeling* which is sufficiently open and flexible for the observer to become a creative being in his/her own right, and, above all, with forming a milieu in which the observer stands to experience something quite ineffable, irreducible to just material quanta and physical qualities, which would succeed in making a lasting impression upon and securing a felt epiphany from that observer.

The experience of looking at and feeling into a given painting, of consciously or unconsciously entering into such a compact, is a very pure form of lived-experience. John Dewey said:

> Experience is the result, the sign, and the reward of that interaction of organism and environment which, when it is carried to the full, is a transformation of interaction into participation and communication.[64]

This is exact for the experience of a Gaucher painting. We interact with the work, and our interaction is soon transformed into a partaking, a participating, a communicating and, far more importantly, a *communing*. And that felt communion, and the union that it implies, is not won easily, neither by the artist nor for the observer.

The anthropoligist and aesthetician Jacques Maquet has further defined this sort of communion in the sense in which it has meaning for Gaucher's endeavour:

> Communion is a deeper and more complete type of relationship between two persons than that resulting from the communication of messages. Communication only involves the cognitive function of the mind, whereas communion is more comprehensive. It is a sharing that gives rise to a broadened identity: beholder and creator constitute a "we." The "we" is extended to other beholders who respond to the same work. They too have been through corresponding experiences.

> A nonorganized set of kindred minds is generated on the basis
> of experiences consonant with each other and with the creator's
> own experiences.[65]

The experiences we commune with are "deep but undefined, important to self but inchoate"; that is, it is not necessary to define them with
any exacting rigour, the multiplicity of meanings implicit in these
paintings in terms of interpretations does not require any straitjacketed
symmetry of experience between artist and observer. While Maquet
insists "the original experience reflected by the work must be respected,"
it is respected only because it corresponds to an experience of our
own.[66] What observer has not, after all, at one time or other, experienced a real feeling of awe, if not in front of a tomb edifice in the Valley
of the Kings, then at least in front of an Egyptian temple reconstructed
at the Metropolitan Museum in New York City? Gaucher has striven
to invest in his paintings a monumentality, and a mastery of colour and
light, that can afford his viewers something deep to commune with,
something that meaningfully corresponds to their own experiences,
even if those experiences are not perfectly synonymous with his own
experiences. But then, those experiences, as Gaucher himself agrees,
are always "deep but *undefined*, important to self but *inchoate*."

Exact definitions, then, are not in question, nor are entirely unprob-
lematical ones. Again, Dewey:

> Since the artist cares in a peculiar way for the phase of expe-
> rience in which union is achieved, he does not shun moments
> of resistance and tension. He rather cultivates them, not for
> their own sake but because of their potentialities, bringing to
> living consciousness an experience that is unified and total.[67]

This is the sort of *unifying* and *totalizing* experience that Yves Gaucher
strives after. And, in this light, *communion* is consummately a difficult
thing to achieve. For it is something that the observer must enter will-
ingly, if at all. Yet, the very ideal of monumentality that Gaucher incor-
porates into his paintings redeems them from being construed as
aesthetic objects pure and simple and manifestly renders them environmental statements that invariably facilitate this felt communion
between object and observer. In this sense, they are akin to the work
of Barnett Newman and Mark Rothko, painters for whom Gaucher has
the utmost respect, because they become somehow larger than they are.
The fact that various critics have discovered affinities between the work
of these artists and that of Gaucher attests to the fact that the authen-
ticity of the communion in question has been widely recognized.

This goes back to what Gaucher said about the experience of the Mayan cities: about radiating something larger than what one is. Similarly, his paintings become environmental concepts realized in paint and on canvas, but *wholly realizable in experience*. And on such a scale that we must continuously reappraise our relationship with them: as minds, as bodies, and, most importantly, as embodied minds, that is, as whole beings. Irradiated with a light that is all openness, and colour that has nothing whatsoever in it of closure, these paintings are chockfull of philosophical intuitions and original experiences.

Assimilating one of Yves Gaucher's current paintings means becoming a creative being and entering into an environmental and empathic compact with it. A compact, then, in which artist and observer are creative partners in relation to which is constituted not only what the painting in question is but what a painting can be in the life-world, the nature of the claim it can stake not only on the receptive optic but on the mind and body of the observer, and the originality of the experience it can offer one, as it unfolds in a temporality that is not that of clock-time but of Bergsonian duration. It is the light in his current paintings that establishes the holding-capacity of their temporality, for the slow transformation of the light is temporally homogenous, and seemingly laden with a plethora of emotional, meditative tonalities. Herein, in organic and spiritual process — in lived-experience pure and simple — lies unity.

His latest work, it seems to me, is as radical as it is strong, and stands as a real landmark in his continuing evolution within the Modernist tradition and, one might suggest, he is one of only a few painters whose work presages a role for abstract painting or opens up a meaningful space for it in postmodernity — perhaps a species of "postmodernist formalism." The remarkable consistency and integrity of Gaucher's oeuvre over the course of the last quarter century shows no signs of tapering off. Indeed, he has upped the ante rather considerably in his newest paintings. Undoubtedly, he will continue to beguile us for a long time to come.

NOTES

1. John Dewey, *Art as Experience* (New York: G.P. Putnam's Sons, 1958), p. 294
2. Conversation with the artist, January 14, 1989.
3. Ibid.
4. Ibid.
5. Ibid.
6. Ibid.
7. Dewey, *Art as Experience*, p. 253.
8. Bryan Robertson, "Yves Gaucher: Eminence Grise at Edinburgh" in *The London Spectator*, August 23, 1968.
9. Emmanuel Levinas, *The Theory of Intuition in Husserl's Phenomenology*, translated by André Orianne (Evanston: Northwestern University Press, 1973), p. 142.
10. Conversation with the artist, December, 1988.
11. Yves Gaucher, transcript of a videotaped interview with Chris Youngs, 1974.
12. Dewey, *Art as Experience*, p. 147.
13. Cited in Roald Nasgaard, *Yves Gaucher: A 15 Year Perspective* (Toronto: The Art Gallery of Ontario, 1978), p. 115.
14. Conversation with the artist, January 14, 1989.
15. Yves Gaucher, "Statement" (Toronto: Galerie Moos, 1966), broadsheet.
16. Ibid.
17. Ibid.
18. Mikel Dufrenne, *The Phenomenology of Aesthetic Experience* (Evanston: Northwestern University Press, 1974), pp. 291-292.
19. Rudolf Arnheim, *The Power of the Center: A Study of Composition in the Visual Arts* rev. ed. (Berkeley: University of California Press, 1982), pp.10-11.
20. Erazim Kohak, *Idea & Experience: Edmund Husserl's Project of Phenomenology in Ideas I* (Chicago: The University of Chicago Press, 1978), p. 78.
21. Ibid.
22. Conversation with the artist, December, 1988
23. Yves Gaucher, cited in Anne Brodsky, "Notice also Silent Sounds, the new work of Yves Gaucher," *artscanada*, XXV, 2, 118/119 (June, 1968), p. 21.
24. Yves Gaucher, cited in David Silcox, "Yves Gaucher" *Canadian Art Today*, ed. William Townsend, *Studio International*, 1970, 27.
25. Conversation with the artist, January 14, 1989.
26. Yves Gaucher, in taped interview with Virgil Hammock, Nov. 18, 1973.
27. Nasgaard, p. 20.
28. Conversation with the artist, December, 1988.
29. Nasgaard, p. 20
30. Nasgaard, pp. 24-25.
31. Doris Shadbolt, "Introduction," *Yves Gaucher* (Vancouver: The Vancouver Art Gallery, 1969). n.p.
32. Conversation with the artist, January 14, 1989.
33. Willam Epstein, *Varieties of Perceptual Learning* (New York: McGraw-Hill Book Company, 1967), pp. 56-63.
34. Gerald Needham, "Painting for Open Space," *artscanada*, 228/229, August/September 1979, p. 19.

35. Nasgaard, p. 57.

36. Ibid., p. 57.

37. Ibid., pp. 58-60.

38. François-Marc Gagnon, "Gaucher," in *16 Quebec Painters in their Milieu,* Vie des Arts Society, 1978, p. 48.

39. Nasgaard., p. 73.

40. Doris Shadbolt, "Introduction" to *Transitions* folio of 8 original lithographs, (Montreal: Galerie Godard-Lefort, 1967),

41. Ibid.

42. Bryan Robertson, *op. cit.*

43. Youngs interview.

44. Dore Ashton, "Yves Gaucher at the New York Cultural Center," *artscanada,* vol. 22, no. 2, June 1975, p. 81.

45. Nasgaard, p. 99.

46. Ibid.

47. Nasgaard, p. 107.

48. Conversation with the artist, January 14, 1989.

49. Conversation with the artist, January 14, 1989.

50. Nasgaard, p. 109.

51. Yves Gaucher, cited in Youngs interview.

52. Nasgaard, p. 111.

53. Ibid.

54. Ibid., p. 121.

55. Ibid., pp. 121-125.

56. Conversation with the artist, January 14, 1989.

57. Rosalind Krauss, "On Frontality" in *The Great Decade of American Abstraction: Modernist Art 1960 to 1970* (Houston: The Museum of Fine Arts, Houston, 1974), p. 89.

58. Ibid., p. 89.

59. Albert Barnes, *The Art of Painting* (Greenwich, Connecticut: The Barnes Foundation Press, 1948), p. 227.

60. Martin Pops, *Vermeer: Consciousness and the Chamber of Being* (Ann Arbor, Michigan: UMI Research Press, 1984), p. 26.

61. M.E. Chevreul, *The Principles of Harmony and Contrast of Colours,* introduction and notes by Faber Birren (New York: Van Nostrand Reinhold Company, 1981), p. 97.

62. Bernhard Kerber, "Dieter Jung" in *Dieter Jung: Paintings/Drawings/Holograms* (New York: Goethe House, Poindexter Gallery, AM Sachs Gallery, 1982), p. 23.

63. Irving Sandler, *The Triumph of American Painting: A History of Abstract Expressionism* (New York: Harper & Row), p. 154.

64. John Dewey, *Art as Experience,* p. 22.

65. Jacques Maquet, *The Aesthetic Experience: An Anthropologist Looks at the Visual Arts* (New Haven: Yale University Press, 1986), p. 158.

66. Ibid., p. 159.

67. Dewey, *op. cit.,* p. 15.

SELECTED SOLO EXHIBITIONS

1957
Galerie l'Echange, Montreal

1963
Galerie Agnes Lefort, Montreal
Gallery Moos, Toronto
Benjamin Galleries, Chicago
Martha Jackson Gallery, New York

1965
Galerie Agnes Lefort, Montreal

1966
Winnipeg Art Gallery, Winnipeg
Gallery Moos, Toronto
Martha Jackson Gallery, New York
International Selection of Prints, Prague, Czechoslovakia

1967
Galerie Agnes Lefort, Montreal
Winnipeg Art Gallery, Winnipeg

1969
Yves Gaucher, Vancouver Art Gallery, Vancouver; Edmonton Art Gallery, Edmonton; Whitechapel Art Gallery, London, England
Galerie Godard-Lefort, Montreal

1970
Sir George Williams University, Montreal
Galerie Moos, Toronto

1971
University of Manitoba, Winnipeg

1972
Galerie Godard-Lefort, Montreal
Marlborough-Godard Gallery, Toronto

1973
Galerie Marlborough-Godard, Montreal

1975

The New York Cultural Center, New York
Marlborough-Godard Gallery, Toronto

1976

Yves Gaucher: Perspective 1963-1976, Musée d'art contemporain, Montreal

1977

Mira Godard Gallery, Toronto

1978

Traveling Exhibition organized by External Affairs Ministry,
Washington, D.C.

1979

Waddington Galleries, Toronto
Yves Gaucher: A Fifteen-Year Perspective 1963-1978, The Art Gallery of Ontario,
Toronto; Glenbow Museum, Calgary

1980

Yves Gaucher: Les Jericho, Musée d'art contemporain,
Montreal

1982

Mural Installation, Nova Corporation, Calgary

1983

Centre Culturel du Canada, Paris, France
Canada House, London, England
Canadian Cultural Centre, Brussels, Belgium

1985

Olga Korper Gallery, Toronto

1986

Galerie Esperanza, Montreal
Olga Korper Gallery, Toronto

1987

Mural installation, Cineplex Odeon, Washington, D.C.

1988
Olga Korper Gallery, Toronto

1989
Olga Korper Gallery, Toronto
49th Parallel Centre for Canadian Contemporary Art, New York

SELECTED GROUP EXHIBITIONS

1960
La Relève, Montreal, Quebec
Le 3e Salon de la Jeune Peinture, Montreal

1961
La Biennale de Paris
IV International Graphics Exhibition, Ljubljana, Yugoslavia

1962
VIIth International Graphics Exhibition, Lugano, Switzerland
International Biennial Exhibition of Prints, Tokyo, Japan
10 Canadian Printmakers, Pratt Institute, New York
Canadian Art Touring Exhibit, Africa
Contemporary Canadian Art, Albright-Knox Art Gallery, Buffalo
Galerie Agnes Lefort, Montreal (with Albert Dumouchel)

1963
Contemporary Art of the Americas and Spain, Madrid, Spain
Junge Kunst der Welt, Vienna, Austria
International Print Exhibition, Osaka, Japan
Vth International Graphics Exhibition, Ljubljana, Yugoslavia
International Collection of Prints, Albertina Museum, Vienna, Austria
1st American Biennial of Prints, Santiago, Chile
Members' Loan Gallery Acquisitions, Albright-Knox Art Gallery, Buffalo

1964
Contemporary Painters as Printmakers, Museum of Modern Art, New York
International Triennial of Coloured Graphic Prints, Grenchen, Switzerland
Canadian Printmakers, Lima, Peru

1965

Art To-Day, Albright-Knox Art Gallery, Buffalo
Vibrations II, Martha Jackson Gallery, New York
The Deceived Eye, Fort Worth Art Center, Fort Worth, Texas
Optics, Illusion and Art, University of Kansas, Lawrence
Optics and Kinetics, Ohio State University, Columbus
I plus II equals Three, University of Texas, Austin
VIth International Biennial of Prints, Ljubljana, Yugoslavia

1966

International Selection of Prints, Museum of Modern Art, Czechoslovakia
1st International Biennial of Prints, Crakow, Poland
XXXIII Venice Bienale

1967

Young International Artists, Tokyo, Japan
Canada '67, Institute of Contemporary Art, Boston
Carnegie International, Pittsburgh
Expo '67, Montreal

1968

Canada 101, Edinburgh Festival, Scotland
Canada — Art d'Aujourd'hui, Palais des Beaux-Arts, Brussels, Belgium

1969

Homage to Silence, Innsbruck, Austria
VII International Dibuix Joan Miro, Barcelona, Spain
19 Canadian Artists, Paris, Rome, Geneva

1970

Drawings Reconsidered, Institute of Contemporary Art, Boston
Expo '70, Osaka, Japan
Grands Formats, Musée d'art contemporain, Montreal

1974

Aspects of Canadian Art, Members' Gallery, Albright-Knox Art Gallery, Buffalo
Thirteen Artists from Marlborough-Godard, Marlborough Gallery, New York

1975

Gagnon, Gaucher, McEwen, Mount Allison University, Sackville, New Brunswick

1976

3 Générations d'Art Québécois, Musée d'art contemporain, Montreal
Perspective 1963-1976, Musée d'art contemporain, Montreal
111 Dessins du Québec, Musée d'art contemporain, Montreal

1977

2nd Exhibition of Works on Paper, Dalhousie University, Halifax
Tableaux Importants du Québec, Galerie B, Montreal

1978

Travelling Exhibition, organized by External Affairs Ministry,
Washington, D.C.
Modern Painting in Canada, Edmonton Art Gallery, Edmonton
Yves Gaucher and Christopher Pratt, A Touring Exhibition of Prints, The Vancouver
Art Gallery, Vancouver

1980

La Semaine de la Gravure, Graff, Montreal
A Canadian Survey, Art Gallery of Ontario, Toronto
Canadian Printmaking, Tokyo, Japan

1981

Contemporary Canadian Painting, Adelphi University, New York, NY
Guest Artists, Yajima Galerie, Montreal
6 Canadian Artists, Montreal Museum Acquisitions Committee, Montreal
A Canadian Survey, Toronto-Dominion Bank Touring Exhibition

1982

Photographs by Artists, Galerie France Morin, Montreal
Recent Canadian Prints, Art Gallery of Ontario, Toronto

1983

International Graphics, Galleria Fenici, Valletta, Malta
Major Paintings of Yesterday and Today, Galerie Michel Tetreault, Montreal

1984

100 Years of Canadian Art, National Gallery of Canada, Ottawa
Masterpieces from the Sixties, Don Stewart Gallery, Montreal
Canadian Paintings, 49th Parallel Gallery, New York
Oeuvres Importantes de Maîtres Québécois, Waddington & Gorce Gallery, Montreal
Collection du Musée du Québec, Quebec

1985

20 ans du MAC, Musée d'art contemporain, Montreal
Concordia University Faculty Show, Concordia University, Montreal
Présence de la Peinture Canadienne, Centre Culturel Canadien, Paris, France
Post-War Canadian Art Exhibited in Swiss Museums,
Swiss Bank Corporation (Canada), Toronto
Olga Korper Gallery, Toronto

1986

"FOKUS" Kanadische Kunst, Kohlnmesse, Germany
Cologne Art Fair, Cologne, Germany
20 ans de Graff, Musée d'art contemporain, Montreal
50 years of Contemporary Canadian Art, 49th Parallel, New York
Galerie Esperanza, Montreal

1987

A Propos d'une Peinture des Années Soixante, Musée d'art contemporain, Montreal
Olga Korper Gallery, Toronto
Gravures d'Hier et Aujourd'hui, Galerie 13, Montreal
Works from 1945 to 1965, Galerie Don Stewart, Montreal
Canadian Printshops, MacDonald Stewart Art Centre, Guelph (and travel)
Painting the Town, national outdoor billboard exhibition, sponsored by The
Manufacturers' Life Insurance Co., shown in Toronto, Montreal, Vancouver,
Calgary, Halifax, St. John's
Chicago Art Fair, Chicago
Cologne Art Fair, Cologne, Germany

1988

L'Artiste au Jardin, Musée régional de Rimouski, Rimouski, Quebec
Quebec Focus; Art Gallery of Ontario, Art Sales & Rental Gallery, Toronto
Olga Korper Gallery, Toronto
Waddington & Gorce Gallery, Montreal
Galerie Daniel, Montreal

1989

Living Impressions, Art Gallery of Hamilton, Hamilton
Montreal Painting of the 1960s, American Society Art Gallery, New York
L'Histoire et la Mémoire, Musée d'art contemporain, Montreal

SELECTED BIBLIOGRAPHY

1957

Chicoine, René. "Formes et Couleurs: Linos, encres et graphisme," *Le Devoir* (29 mars, 1957), (rev. Galerie l'Echange).

De Repentigny, Rodolphe. "Linos de Gaucher et encres par Faucher," *La Presse* (mars 1957), (rev. Galerie l'Echange).

1960

De Repentigny, Françoise. "La Relève? de qui, de quoi?" *Le Devoir* (13 fevrier, 1960).

_____. "Venor: la révélation du 3e Salon de la Jeune Peinture," *Le Devoir* (24 mars, 1960).

1961

Martin, Paul. "Avec ses cuivres martelés, Yves Gaucher donne une troisième dimension à la gravure," *Le Nouveau Journal* (25 novembre, 1961).

Sarrazin, Jean. "Graveurs Canadiens et Etrangers," *Le Nouveau Journal* (juin 1961), (rev. Galerie Agnes Lefort).

1962

"The Arts — The Printmakers," *Time, LXXX:* 26 (December 28, 1962), 8-10.

Fenwick, Kathleen. "Gaucher," *Canadian Art*, 19:2 (March/April, 1962), 122-123.

Jasmin, Claude. "Dumouchel and Gaucher at the Galerie Agnes Lefort, Montreal," *Canadian Art*, 19:5 (September/October, 1962), 323-324.

1963

Auersberg, Ruth. "Yves Gaucher at the Galerie Agnes Lefort, Montreal," *Canadian Art*, 20:6 (November/December, 1963), 318-319.

Ayre, Robert. "Two Canadian Printmakers," *The Star* (June 8, 1963), (rev. Galerie Agnes Lefort).

E[dgar], N[atalie], "Reviews & Previews," *Art News*, 62:8 (December 1963), 56, (rev. Martha Jackson Gallery).

Jasmin, Claude, "Yves Gaucher," *La Presse* (15 juin, 1963).

Lamy, Laurent, "Gaucher, à la Galerie Agnes Lefort," *Le Devoir* (8 juin, 1963).

1964

"Gaucher Print Wins Prize," *The Gazette* (November 11, 1964).

"Prix remporté par un graveur canadien Yves Gaucher," *Le Devoir* (2 juin 1964).

Heard, Raymond. "Yves Gaucher: The Energy of Color," *The Montreal Star* (November 7, 1964).

Rose, Barbara. "Yves Gaucher at the Martha Jackson Gallery, New York," *Canadian Art*, 21:2 (March/April 1964), 63.

1965

Cutler, May Ebbitt. "Yves Gaucher," *Canadian Art*, 22:4 (September/October 1965), 26-28.
Jasmin, Claude, "Yves Gaucher: 'L'expressif, je n'y crois plus,'" *La Presse* (1 mars, 1965).
_____. "Yves Gaucher: 'op art' et désincarnation," *La Presse* (24 avril, 1965), (rev. Galerie Agnes Lefort).
Montbizon, Rea. "Danses Carrées," *The Gazette* (April 29, 1965), (rev. Galerie Agnes Lefort).

1966

Balfour, Lisa. "Reaching Out For New Experiences," *Montreal Star* (June 11, 1966).
Folch, Jacques. "Yves Gaucher," *Vie des Arts*, no. 41, Winter, 1965-66, 40-43.
Harper, Russell J. *Painting in Canada, A History.* Toronto: University of Toronto Press, 1966.
New York, The Martha Jackson Gallery, *Yves Gaucher*, September-October, 1966.
Silcox, David P. "Canadian Art in the Sixties," *Canadian Art* 23:1 (January, 1966), 55-61.
Toronto, Gallery Moos Ltd. *Yves Gaucher*, April 1966 (text by Gaucher).
Venice, XXXIII Bienale de Venezia, *Canada '66*, 1966 (intro. Willem A. Blom).
W[aldman], D[iane]. "Reviews & Previews," *Art News*, 65:5 (September 1966), 14, 17 (rev. Martha Jackson).

1967

Ayre, Robert. "Yves Gaucher's Optical 'Ragas,'" *The Montreal Star* (May 16, 1967), (rev. Galerie Agnes Lefort).
Gaulin, Manon. "Toward Serenity," *Time*, (Can. ed.), May 26, 1967, 9.
Gladu, Paul. "Yves Gaucher — The Search for Simplicity," *The Gazette* (May 20, 1967).
Lord, Barry. "Discover Canada: Canadian Art Since 1940," *Art in America*, 55:3 (May/June 1967), 78-84.
R[obillard], Y[ves]. "Gaucher et les champs énergétiques de la couleur," *La Presse* (13 mai, 1967), (rev. Galerie Agnes Lefort).
Shadbolt, Doris. Textplate, *Transitions*, Album of 8 Original Lithographs, Galerie Godard-Lefort, Montreal, 1967.
The Winnipeg Art Gallery. *Yves Gaucher*, April 29-May 21, 1967 (intro. Dorothy Cameron).
Zemel, Carol. "Montreal spring '67: in the galleries," *Artscanada*, xxiv 6/7, 109-110 (June/July 1967), 2 (rev. Galerie Agnes Lefort).

1968

"Sondage 68' demain au Musée," *La Presse* (7 mars, 1968).
"Sondage 68': premier prix a Yves Gaucher," *La Presse* (8 mars, 1968).

Ayre, Robert, "Gaucher tops art contest," *The Montreal Star* (March 8, 1968).

Brodzky, Anne. "Notice Also Silent Sounds, the New Work of Yves Gaucher," *Artscanada*, xxv: 2, 118-119 (June, 1968), 21-23.

MacDonald, Colin, S. *Dictionary of Canadian Artists*, vol. 2. Ottawa: Canadian Paperbacks, 1968.

Robertson, Bryan. "Eminence grise at Edinburgh," *Spectator*, 221-7313 (August 23, 1968), 267.

Thompson, David. "A Canadian scene: 3," *Studio International*, 176:906 (December 1968), 242-245.

1969

Ayre, Robert. "Gaucher — the philosophic calm of pure painting," *The Montreal Star* (January 4, 1969), (rev. Galerie Godard-Lefort).

Blakeston, Oswell. "Yves Gaucher: Whitechapel Art Gallery," *Arts Review* (October 5, 1969).

Brett, Guy. "Gaucher's quiet art," *The Times* (November 5, 1969), (rev. Whitechapel Gallery).

Bruce-Milne, Marjorie. "Gaucher: the sound of gray," *The Christian Science Monitor* (November 3, 1969), (rev. Whitechapel Gallery).

Chandler, John Noel. "Dialogue at an exhibition of Yves Gaucher's Grey Paintings," *Artscanada*, xxvi: 5, 136-137 (October, 1969), 3-6, (rev. Vancouver Art Gallery).

Gosling, Nigel. "A kind of silence," *The Observer Review* (October 26, 1969), (rev. Whitechapel Gallery).

Lowndes, Joan. "Man Who Paints the Sound of Silence," *The Province* (Vancouver), April 18, 1969.

_____. "Gaucher— Metaphor for Contemporary Music," *The Province* (Vancouver), May 2, 1969, (rev. Vancouver Art Gallery).

Millet, Robert. "Gaucher: manipuler avec l'oeil," *Le Magazine Maclean*, 9:89 (octobre 1969), 89.

Russell, John. "Art," *The Sunday Times* (October 26, 1969), (rev. Whitechapel Gallery).

Salvesen, Christopher. "Greys," *The Listener*, v. 82:2116 (October 16, 1969), 536, (rev. Whitechapel Gallery).

Silcox, David. "Yves Gaucher," *Studio International*, 177:908 (February 1969), 76-77.

Thériault, Normand. "Gaucher: prélude à une exposition," *La Presse* (4 fevrier, 1969), (rev. Galerie Godard-Lefort).

"Yves Gaucher, Galerie Godard-Lefort," *Artscanada*, xxvi:I, 128/129 (February 1969), 45.

The Vancouver Art Gallery. *Yves Gaucher* (intro. Doris Shadbolt).

Whittet, G.S. "Dans les galeries londoniennes," *Le Monde* (30 octobre, 1969), (rev. Whitechapel Gallery).

1970

Bardo, Arthur. "Gaucher graphics, Coward paintings," *The Montreal Star* (February 12, 1970), (rev. Sir George Williams University).

Bernier, Thérèse. "Revue de l'année 1969 dans le domaine artistique: Arts plastiques," *Le Devoir* (5 janvier, 1970).

Capper, Ann. "Yves Gaucher exhibit returns," *The Gazette* (February 14, 1970), (rev. Sir George Williams University).

Chandler, John Noel. "Drawing reconsidered," *Artscanada*, v. 27:148-149 (October 1970), 56.

Raymond, Marie. "Yves Gaucher Expose à Londres," *Vie des Arts*, no. 57 (hiver 1969-1970), 56.

Thériault, Normand. "L'art du signe," *La Presse* (February 7, 1970), (rev. Sir George Williams University).

1971

Gopnik, Myrna and Irwin. "Seeing is believing: Yves Gaucher's new paintings," *Artscanada*, xxviii: 5, 160-161 (October/November 1971), 32-33.

1972

Dault, G.M. "Notes on recent shows — some Toronto news," *Artscanada*, xxix: 2, 166-168 (February-May 1972), 91-94.

Kirkman, Terry and Judy Heviz. "Gaucher alters his style," *The Montreal Star* (21 janvier, 1972).

Kritzwiser, Kay. "Yves Gaucher," *The Globe and Mail* (April 8, 1972), (rev. Marlborough-Godard Gallery, Toronto).

Weiler, Merike. "Artist Yves Gaucher a master of lyrical understatement," *The Toronto Star* (April 19, 1972), (rev. Marlborough-Godard Gallery, Toronto).

White, Michael. "The quiet voice of Yves Gaucher, painter," *The Gazette* (January 22, 172), (rev. Galerie Godard-Lefort).

Withrow, William. *Contemporary Canadian Painting*. Toronto: McClelland and Stewart Limited, 1972.

1973

Arbec, Jules. "Variations," *Le Devoir* (2 avril, 1973), (rev. Galerie Marlborough-Godard, Montreal).

Kirby, W.J.G. *A Discussion of Five Canadian Painters in the Context of the Artistic and Critical Sensibility of the 1960's*. M.A. Thesis, University of British Columbia, 1973.

Ragon, Michel. "Yves Gaucher: rêverie de l'absolu," *Vie des Arts*, xvii: 70 (Printemps, 1973), 28-33.

1975

Ashton, Dore. "Yves Gaucher at the New York Cultural Centre," *Artscanada*, xxxii:2, 198-199 (June 1975), 81.

The New York Cultural Centre. *Yves Gaucher*, March 13-April 27, 1975 (intro. Mario Amaya).

James, Geoffrey. "Yves Gaucher's Silent Sounds," *Time* (Can. ed.), (March 24, 1975), 12-14, (rev. New York Cultural Center).

1976

Bogardi, George. "Yves Gaucher," *The Montreal Star* (October 16, 1976), (rev. Musée d'art contemporain).

Yves Gaucher, Le Centre de documentation Yvon Boulerice, Montreal, 1976 (80 slides/diapositives, texts by J.N. Chandler, N. Thériault, M. Greenwood).

Musée d'art contemporain, Montreal. *Perspective 1963-1976, Yves Gaucher: Peintures et gravures*, le 7 octobre-le 7 novembre, 1976 (intro. Alain Parent).

Parent, Alain. *111 Dessins du Québec*, Musée d'art contemporain, Montreal, 1976.

Toupin, Gilles. "Yves Gaucher: un plongeon dans la couleur," *La Presse* (23 octobre 1976), (rev. Musée d'art contemporain).

Saint Martin, Fernande. *Trois Générations d'Art Québécois*, Musée d'art contemporain, Montreal, 1976.

1977

Greenwood, Michael. "Yves Gaucher," *Artscanada*, xxxiv:2, 214-215 (May/June 1977), 53.

Tessèydre, Bernard. "Couleur et Structure chez un Peintre Contemporain de Montréal," *Atelier*, 5:3, 1977 (1965).

Thériault, Normand. "The Last Picture Shown," *Parachute*, 6 (Spring 1977), 38-44.

Yves Gaucher & Christopher Pratt: A Touring Exhibition of Prints, organized by the Vancouver Art Gallery in collaboration with the Mira Godard Gallery, Toronto, April 23-May 29, 1977 (intro. Ann Morrison).

1978

Fenton, Terry and Karen Wilkin. *Modern Painting in Canada*. Edmonton: The Edmonton Art Gallery, 1978.

Gagnon, François-Marc. *16 Artistes Quebecois dans leur Milieu/16 Quebec Painters in their Milieu*. Montreal: Vie des Arts Society, 1978.

Mellen, Peter. *Landmarks of Canadian Art*. Toronto: McClelland and Stewart Limited, 1978.

1979

Bogardi, George. "Yves Gaucher at the AGO," *The Montreal Star* (April 18, 1979).

Brooks, J. "Exhibition Pivots on Perception," *Calgary Sunday Sun* (July 27, 1979).

Dault, G.M. "Yves Gaucher at AGO," *Toronto Star* (April 17, 1979).

Gordon, T. "Perspective d'Yves Gaucher," *Vie des Arts*, Summer 1979.

Hodgson, T. *Artists' Review* (Toronto), Vol. 2 (November 1979).

Mays, John B. "Music and Silence on Canvas," *Macleans*, April 16, 1979.

Monk, Philip. "Yves Gaucher: Eyesight and Temporality" *Parachute*, No. 16 (Fall 1979).

Nasgaard, Roald. *Yves Gaucher: A Fifteen-Year Perspective* (catalogue) Art Gallery of Ontario, 1979.

Needham, G. "Yves Gaucher: Painting for Open Space," *Artscanada*, 228/229 (August/September 1979).

Viau, R. "Yves Gaucher à Toronto," *Le Devoir*, April 25, 1979.

Tousley, N. "Gaucher: a 15-year Perspective," *Calgary Herald* (September 16, 1979).

Tousley, N. "Gaucher Talks Again at Glenbow," *Calgary Herald* (October 18, 1979).

Vastokas, J.M. "Roots of Abstraction: An Introduction," *Artscanada*, 36:2-23 (May/June 1979).

1980

Chandler, J.N. "Dialogue at an Exhibition," *Artscanada*, Summer 1980.

1981

Practor, C. *Contemporary Music of the 20th Century.* Toronto: University of Toronto Press, 1981.

Clark, James. *The Problem of Fundamental Ontology III.* Toronto: Limits, 1981.

1983

Visions: Contemporary Art in Canada. ed. Robert Bringhurst, Geoffrey James, Russell Keziere and Doris Shadbolt. Vancouver/Toronto: Douglas & McIntyre, 1983.

Dault, G.M. *A Primer of Canadan Abstraction,* D.M.I., Toronto.

Le Musée du Québec: *50 Années d'acquisition Québec,* Quebec 1983.

Burnett, D. and Schiff, M. *Contemporary Canadian Art.* Edmonton: Hurtig Publications, 1983.

J.J.L. "Yves Gaucher à Paris." *Nouvelles Littéraires,* Paris, May 19, 1983.

"Yves Gaucher," *Liberation,* Paris, May 2, 1983.

"Yves Gaucher," *Arts Actions,* Paris, May 1983.

"Yves Gaucher," *Nouvelles de l'Estampe,* Paris, May 1983.

Couturier, E. "Yves Gaucher," *Art Press,* Paris, June 1983.

"Yves Gaucher," *Canada d'Aujourd'hui,* Paris, July 1983.

"Yves Gaucher," *Beaux-Arts Magazine,* Paris, May 1983.

Nasgaard, R. *Yves Gaucher: Paintings and Etchings,* exhibition catalogue, Centre Cultural du Canada, Paris, France, Canada House, London, England, Canadian Cultural Centre, Brussels, Belgium.

1985

Mays, John B. "The Welcome Return of Yves Gaucher," *The Globe and Mail* (March 9, 1985).

1986

Gilbert, Jean-Pierre. "Interview with Yves Gaucher," *ETC* (Montreal), No. 1.
"Gaucher et Gamoy: Des Perspectives Contradictoiries," *Le Devoir* (March 22, 1986).
Sabbath, Lawrence. "Gaucher at Esperanza," *The Montreal Gazette* (March 22, 1986).
Corbeil, Carole. "Gaucher Works on Paper at Olga Korper Gallery," *The Globe and Mail* (April 17, 1986).
de Roussan, Jacques. "Yves Gaucher, ou la réalité de la perception," *Vie des Arts*, 123 (June 1986).

1987

Murray, Joan. *The Best Contemporary Canadian Art*. Edmonton: Hurtig Publishers, 1987.
Musée d'art contemporain, Montreal. *A Propos une Peinture des Années Soixante: Ewen, Gagnon, Gaucher, Hurtubise, McEwen,* 1987.
Kirtzwiser, Kay. "Artists Get High on Manufacturers' Centennial," *The Globe and Mail* (June 29, 1987).
Painting the Town, catalogue for national outdoor billboard exhibition, sponsored by The Manufacturers' Life Insurance Co.

1988

Musée Regional de Rimouski. *L'artiste au Jardin.* Rimouski, Quebec
"Perceiving Painting Through the Pores," *Now Magazine,* Toronto, March 10, 1988.
Brackett, Donald. "Yves Gaucher and Christopher Kier," *Arts Report,* (Toronto), March 8, 1988.
Thériault, Normand. "Art: Style over Story," *Forces,* no. 84 (Winter, 1988).
Reid, Dennis. *A Concise History of Canadian Painting,* revised ed. Toronto: Oxford University Press, 1988.

1989

Burnett, David. *Cineplex Odeon, The First Ten Years: A Celebration of Contemporary Canadian Art.* Toronto: Cineplex Odeon, 1989.
Thériault, Marie-Josée. *Rencontres/Encuentros.* Montreal: Editions Sans Nom, 1989.
Gilbert, Jean-Pierre and Lebel, Susan. "Interview with Yves Gaucher," *ETC* (Montreal), No. 8 (Spring 1989).

Video Productions

TV Ontario, Producer D. Thomson, *Visions: Canadian Art since 1950* (Yves Gaucher, Charles Gagnon and Pierre Gauvreau), duration 30 minutes.
Letocha, Louise, Musée d'art contemporain Montréal, 1976 (15 minutes).
Youngs, Christopher, Yves Gaucher, Mount Allison University, N.B. (60 minutes), 1975.
Kinley, Lohn: Productions E.T.V. Ontario (30 minutes), 1972.